Notes of a Director

BOOKS OF THE THEATRE SERIES

H. D. Albright, General Editor

Number 7

A Rare Books of the Theatre project of the
American Educational Theatre Association

Alexander Tairov

Notes
of a Director

By
ALEXANDER   TAIROV

Translated, and with an introduction by
WILLIAM KUHLKE

UNIVERSITY OF MIAMI PRESS
Coral Gables, Florida

Credit is hereby gratefully acknowledged for photographs on the following pages: fron-
tispiece, TASS from SOVFOTO; pp. 60, 61, 180 from KNIGA O KAMERNO TEATRE
by Konstantine Derzhavin; pp. 83, 113 (top), 127, 128, 130 (top) from THE RUSSIAN
THEATRE by René Fülöp-Miller and Joseph Gregor; p. 113 (bottom) from THE
RUSSIAN THEATRE by Oliver Saylor; p. 121 (top) from National Library, Vienna;
pp. 121 (bottom), 130 (bottom), 131 from DAS ENTFESSELTE THEATER, by
Alexander Tairov; p. 83 from THE THEATRE IN A CHANGING EUROPE by Thomas
H. Dickinson and others. Copyright 1937 by Holt, Rinehart and Winston, Inc. Copy-
right (C) 1965 by Thomas H. Dickinson. Holt, Rinehart and Winston, Inc., Publisher.

For Alice Koonen

— *Alexander Tairov*

Contents

Foreword *13*

Translator's Introduction *17*

I *Pro Domo Sua* *39*

II Dilettantism and Professional Excellence *66*

III The Actor's Internal Technique *73*

IV The Actor's External Technique *81*

V The Director *90*

VI The Role of Literature in the Theatre *96*

VII Music in the Theatre *103*

VIII Scenic Atmosphere *106*

IX Costume *125*

X The Spectator *132*

Notes *145*

Index *151*

Illustrations

Alexander Tairov *frontispiece*

Scene design for *Shakuntala* 60

Alice Koonen as Shakuntala 61

Princess Brambilla 83

Princess Brambilla 84

Famira Kifared 113

Famira Kifared: satyrs carry off menads in bacchanal 113

Salome 120

Salome: model by Alexandra Ekster 121

Salome: the Sadducees 121

Phaedra: the costume itself 127

Costume sketch for *Phaedra* 128

Adrienne Lecouvreur 130

Costume models for *Giroflé-Girofla* 130

Costume models for *Adrienne Lecouvreur* 131

Foreword

As the seventh volume in the Books of the Theatre Series, the editors offer another important work previously unpublished in English: *Notes of a Director,* by Alexander Tairov (Alexander Jakovlevich Kornblit, 1885-1950).

A distinguished director and theorist, Tairov has long deserved to be better known in America. Generator of excitement in an already exciting period for the Russian theatre, he developed what he called a "theatre of synthesis" in his now-famous Chamber (Kamerny) Playhouse. The present volume records the policy-making, the experimentation, and the week-by-week work of the Kamerny's first six years.

As the translator points out in a comprehensive introduction, the Russian theatre of the early century is—for most American students—essentially Stanislavsky's theatre. A more complete picture would include Meyerhold and Vakhtangov, and perhaps others as well. In any case, *Notes of a Director* will help to introduce, and to illuminate, one more facet of the picture for the American reader.

American rights for the volume were arranged through Am-Rus Literary Agency. Photographic acknowledgments are made on the copyright page.

H. D. ALBRIGHT

Editor

Notes of a Director

Introduction

Notes of a Director is the record of the first six years of the Moscow Kamerny Theatre and an organized exposition of the theories which stimulated its foundation and animated its work. The book was first published by the Kamerny Theatre in 1921. It appeared soon after in an authorized German translation as *Das Entfesselte Theater* (Potsdam, 1923). This is its first appearance in English.

At first thought, one would assume that the translation of a work by such a prominent Russian director as Alexander Tairov would be able to stand by itself without the crutch of a lengthy introduction, particularly in the United States. The American theatre has been heavily influenced by its Russian counterpart since the 1920's, not only by visits of touring companies and guest artists, but by emigré artists and teachers who have trained generations of American actors. Indeed, insofar as America has an acting tradition today, it is Stanislavskian—variously interpreted.

As a matter of fact, this preoccupation with Stanislavsky is precisely the problem. For most of us today Stanislavsky *is* the Russian theatre. We know, or think we know, a great deal about the Moscow Art Theatre and its great director, and seldom does a year pass without the appearance of an article or a book which adds to our knowledge of the famous "system." But of the other great innovators of the Russian stage, of Komissarzhevsky and Evreinov (in spite of their long residence in the West), of Meyerhold, Vakhtangov, and Tairov, we are still relatively ignorant.

To be sure, there was a flurry of articles about these men in the 1920's and 1930's, and we have valuable firsthand reports of their work by Huntly Carter, Oliver Saylor, H. W. L. Dana, André Van Gyseghen, and Norris

Houghton. But without their own written body of theory and their personal accounts of its practical application to represent them, the anti-realists quite naturally faded in the shadow of *My Life in Art, An Actor Prepares, Building a Character*, and *Creating a Role*. . . . Not that they were not writing their own manifestoes. Indeed, they were all more prolific publishers at the time than the hesitant and careful Stanislavsky. Meyerhold's *O teatre (On the Theatre)*, Evreinov's *Teatr kak takovoi (The Theatre as Such)* and *Teatr dlia sebia (Theatre for its Own Sake)*, Komissarzhevsky's *Tvorchestvo actera i teoriia Stanislavskogo (The Actor's Creative Work and the Stanislavsky Theory)* and *Teatral'niia preliudii (Theatrical Preludes)*, several articles by Vakhtangov, and Tairov's *Zapiski rezhissera (Notes of a Director)*—all had been published before *My Life in Art* first appeared in 1924. But Stanislavsky was fortunate enough to have his Elizabeth Reynolds Hapgood, and before the rest found a comparable champion-translator, the antipathies of international politics outside and the purges of the thirties within the Soviet Union discouraged our interest in Russian theatre practice.

Ironically, the American theatre today, half a century later, is facing many of the same problems which the great innovators of the Russian theatre were trying to solve. The stifling hold of realism on the stage is once more being challenged by new forms of playwriting as well as by production; decentralization is increasing rapidly, and the need for new schools of acting to train artists for new theatres and new forms of theatre is urgent. And so we find ourselves returning once more to the still untapped reservoir of information about one of the greatest periods of experimentation in the history of Western theatre, not out of mere antiquarian curiosity, but out of a pressing need to profit from the experience of a cadre of theatrical geniuses who faced problems so similar to ours. But before we can profit from their experience, we must now be reminded, however briefly, of the artistic milieu in which their experiments took place—a milieu which has been obscured for most Americans by time and the haze of the Stanislavsky cult.

1

To begin, then, the revolution of the modern theatre in Russia pretty much followed the pattern which had developed in Western Europe. It was initiated by Stanislavsky and Nemirovich-Danchenko as a revolt against the repertory of cheap melodrama, farce, and "pot-boilers" written by hacks to show off certain star actors and actresses, as well as against the unimaginative and stul-

tifying production plans, implemented in woefully inadequate rehearsal sched-
ules by traffic-cop directors and set in stock settings of "Gothic," or "Renaissance," or "rich room," or "poor room." Taking as his models Kronegk, the
Duke of Saxe-Meiningen's authoritarian director, and Shchepkin, the origina-
tor of Russian realistic acting, and stimulated by his work with the plays of
Chekhov, Stanislavsky soon made of the Moscow Art Theatre the greatest of
the realistic theatres and of himself the greatest of realistic directors. But the
seeds sown by Stanislavsky were to reap a harvest of directors, the brilliance
of whose achievements were to rival his own and whose reaction against their
teacher was to lead the anti-realist counterrevolution.

By the time the Moscow Art Theatre had accomplished its brilliantly
successful revolution, the anti-realist reaction was already well developed in
art, literature, ballet, and opera. In 1898, Serghey Diaghilev had founded a
magazine called *The World of Art,* which introduced Russian artists to impressionism, French cubism, and German expressionism. These new ideas had their
first impact on painting, to be sure, but Russian symbolism had already established itself as a school in literature and was publishing its own almanac,
Russian Symbolists (1894). Aestheticism and art-for-art's-sake ran as a strong
undercurrent among artists of the time, in spite of the fact that the spirit of
revolt corresponded to and took support from the gathering force of the political revolution. Bitter disappointment over the disastrous political failures of
1905 seemed to give added impetus to movements in nonrepresentational
art forms, perhaps as a form of escape from the unpalatable realities of
politics. From 1905 on, the world of art and letters exploded with new forms,
violent controversies, and a proliferation of artistic "isms."

Meanwhile, after Chekhov's death in 1904, Stanislavsky began to wonder
if the Art Theatre were working itself into a blind alley in its preoccupation
with realism. He determined to find new modes of theatrical expression in
fantasy and symbolism. In 1905 he set up a studio devoted to this search,
giving its direction to Vsevelod Meyerhold, a former actor in the Art Theatre,
who had left to direct his own productions in the provinces. After six months
the studio was closed, ostensibly for lack of funds. It was also true, however,
that Stanislavsky was disappointed in the work of the studio and dubious
about the direction Meyerhold's experiments were taking. In his productions
of Maeterlinck's *The Death of Tintagiles* and Hauptmann's *Schluck and Jau,*
Meyerhold had subordinated everything to the service of a sharp, visual impression with strong symbolic impact. An oversized bed with an enormous canopy

was designed to evoke a feeling of, rather than to represent, a king's bedroom. The setting of a painter's studio was suggested by a huge canvas across half the stage. Action was accompanied and underscored by music. The actors themselves fit—Stanislavsky no doubt felt they were forced—into the overall rhythmic and visual pattern. Their pure diction and precisely choreographed movement and gestures were perfectly blended with the music and decorations, but their souls were dead—no sense of emotional experiencing emanated from them. There was no sense of real human beings living and suffering. Such, at least, was Stanislavsky's impression.

Stanislavsky returned to realism, experimenting from time to time with the symbolic plays of Andreyev, Maeterlinck, and Ibsen, and eventually found room in the growing organization of the Moscow Art Theatre and its studios for both realism and symbolism—even the theatricalism of Vakhtangov. Meyerhold went to the Komissarzhevskaya Theatre in St. Petersburg, continued his experiments, and became the greatest of the anti-realistic directors and an outspoken critic of Stanislavsky and the Moscow Art Theatre.

2

In the company of the Komissarzhevskaya Theatre at this time was a young law-student-turned-actor by the name of Kornblit, who had taken the stage name of Tairov. Alexander Jakovlevich Kornblit had been born in Romny, in the district of Poltava, June 24, 1885. As the son of a school teacher, he was exposed to the arts from childhood, and he claimed that his interest in the theatre stemmed from having seen a performance of *Faust* by the famous Adelgeit brothers when he was just a boy.

During his attendance at the gymnasium in Kiev, Tairov indulged his fascination for the theatre by haunting the local opera house. In 1904 he enrolled as a law student at the University of Kiev, but his interest in the theatre had grown deeper than that of mere spectator, and in 1905 he joined one of the local companies formed by the energetic entrepreneur Michail Matveevich Borodai. He played Lysander in *A Midsummer Night's Dream* and the Burgomeister in Hauptmann's *The Assumption of Hannele* for Borodai, and then in September of the same year transferred to St. Petersburg to join the company of the newly formed theatre of Vera Komissarzhevskaya. There he came under the influence of Meyerhold, under whose direction he appeared in Maeterlinck's *Sister Beatrice* and Blok's *Balaganchik (The Little Show Booth)*.

Tairov was by this time no longer an eager dilettante but an intense and serious young theatre artist, who had followed avidly with his keen intellect the course of the artistic revolution which was at that time taking place in the Russian capital. Here, at the Komissarzhevskaya Theatre, he had the opportunity to talk and work with the leaders of that revolution: Meyerhold, Blok, Kuzmin, Sologub, Vyacheslav Ivanov, Sapunov, Sudeikin. By the end of a season's work under Meyerhold, however, he had become disillusioned. A theatre which put the decorative principle uppermost and which denied the actor his rightful place as an independently creative artist was not his idea of the theatre of the future. He left the Komissarzhevskaya and joined Gaideburov's Mobile Theatre.

Tairov toured Russia with the Mobile Theatre for two years, first as an actor, later as director (*Hamlet,* Zhulavsky's *Eros and Psyche*). In 1909 he directed a production of Andreyev's *Anathema* in Riga. The next season found him back in St. Petersburg playing Mizgir in Ostrovsky's *The Snow Maiden* at the New Dramatic Theatre. He stayed on in St. Petersburg for one more year, directing Benavente's *Los Interesses creados (The Bonds of Interest)* and Hauptmann's *Gabriel Schellings Flucht (Gabriel Schelling's Flight),* and at the same time, apparently, completing his law studies.

By 1912, then, Tairov had had thorough experience as actor and director both in the theatre of realism and the stylized theatre. Neither had satisfied him. So, casting as it were a plague on both their houses, he left the stage —he thought forever—presumably to practice law. Nevertheless, 1913 found him in Moscow, having been invited by Mardzhanov to stage a pantomime, *The Veil of Pierrette,* for an exciting new enterprise called The Free Theatre.

The Free Theatre went bankrupt after one year, but Tairov came out with profit indeed. He had found there his future wife, Alice Koonen, and the kind of theatre he had been searching for. He called it synthetic theatre.

Why "synthetic"? For two reasons. In the first place, following the example of the Free Theatre, this was to be a theatre which incorporated in one company of actors all the talents usually associated separately with ballet, opera, the circus, and the music hall as well as with the dramatic theatre. Also, following the "new stagecraft," Tairov intended to fuse all the arts of spectacle—scene design, costuming, lighting—into a unified expression of the "atmosphere" of the play. It was also "synthetic" in another, rather more significant way. It sought what was essentially a middle path between Meyerhold and Stanislavsky, avoiding their respective excesses and incorporating in its philosophy and methods certain elements of both systems, elements which, however, were transformed in the process of fusion into a new kind of theatre, a "synthetic" theatre.

3

Since both Stanislavsky and Meyerhold had long careers and continued to revise their viewpoints and experiment with new methods of production to the end of their lives, it is important to an understanding of the significance of Tairov's innovations to establish the positions of these two giants during the period 1904-1920. Only then can Tairov's position and its importance be made clear.

Stanislavsky and Nemirovich-Danchenko had proclaimed their theatre to be *representational,* in contrast to the declamatory *presentational* style of the state theatres at the end of the nineteenth century. The masters of the Moscow Art Theatre looked at a play text as a world complete in itself, and their job was to bring it faithfully to life on the stage. The object was not to present the text to the audience, reinforcing it by means of vocal and bodily inflection, so much as it was to represent the play, and to represent it as an independent entity. In a sense, then, the audience had no direct connection with the production process. Once the company had brought a play faithfully to life on the stage, its task was completed, theoretically at least. The only consideration given to the audience was that one wall of the stage was knocked out, through which it was privileged to observe the world thus represented.

The supreme principle of this representation was truth to life. At first the observance of this principle took the form of rather coarse, external naturalism. Later, through work with the plays of Chekhov particularly, this preoccupation with external detail was superseded by attempts to be more selective, to reveal instead of infinite detail the dominant feature of the environment, and to place even greater emphasis on achieving that inner, psychological realism in the acting performance for which the Art Theatre became famous. His work on Chekhov had confirmed Stanislavsky in his conviction that "in order to make the public listen to the fine shadings of [one's] feelings [one] has to *experience* them intensely."[1]

Stanislavsky proceeded on the premise that the subject of the drama is not physical action but that inner, psychic action which is the core, the mainspring to the things men do and say. He reasoned, then, that the focus of the artist who wants to represent human action should be not on the outward and physical but on that inner, psychic action. In such a theatre, the key to the actor's art becomes his ability to experience the role "spiritually." As Stanislavsky stated, "Nine-tenths of the labour of an actor, nine-tenths of everything lies in beginning to live and feel the role spiritually." [2]

Contrary to the intimations of some of his detractors at the time, including Tairov, Stanislavsky always made a perfectly clear distinction between life and acting. The "sincere," "real" emotional reactions of the actor were always to be recast into patterns dictated by the role. However, Stanislavsky was fond of saying that the greatest artist was nature. Once, during a tour to Kiev, while strolling in a park with some of the members of his company, he was persuaded to play a scene from *A Month in the Country* on one of the park benches. Dismayed by the incongruity and falseness of their acting in this real setting, he broke off and could not continue. Later, describing that experience, he said:

> I stopped, because I could not continue my false and theatrical pose. All that I had done seemed untrue to nature, to reality. . . . The trees, the air, the sun hinted to us of such real, beautiful and artistic truth which cannot, because of its aestheticism, be compared to that which is created in us by the dead wings of a theatre. . . . This artistic truth, hinted to us by nature, is incomparably more aesthetic and more beautiful, and what is even more important, more scenic than that relative truth and theatrical conventionality with which it is the habit to limit theatrical creativeness. [3]

Such a point of view bound Stanislavsky in those days inevitably to the theatre of illusion. [4] It allowed him to investigate symbolism and impressionism because to him these were illusionistic styles. In the first the emphasis was on what lay behind the phenomena apparent to the physical senses; in the second it was on the way the senses actually perceive natural phenomena. But to Stanislavsky both styles still focused on nature, however perceived, and their goal was in one form or another to recreate an illusion of natural beauty and truth.

This point of view, of course, prevented him from conceding the validity of the theatricalist, presentational theatre. Art to him was of necessity imitative. Its creative goal was to approximate the work of the highest artist, nature. Any movement away from this goal would have been a movement away from truth and beauty. He had succeeded in his production plan when, as Nemirovich-Danchenko put it, "life unfolded in such frank simplicity that the

auditors seemed almost embarrassed to be present; it was as if they eaves-
dropped behind a door or peeped through a window."[5]

4

In 1911 Stanislavsky had founded the First Studio under the leadership of
Sulerzhitsky and assigned to it the task of developing the Stanislavsky system
and of establishing an intimate theatre which would permit this system to
work to best advantage. In the studio's production of Dickens' *The Cricket on
the Hearth* in 1912, Stanislavsky saw for the first time, to his own satisfaction
at least, "those deep and heart-felt notes of superconscious feeling" in the
"measure and form" in which he had dreamed of them but could not realize
in the larger theatre, where the actors had to strain theatrically to be heard.
Meyerhold, criticizing the play in his *Journal of Doctor Dapertutto,* condemned it and the intimate theatre as sops to morbid human curiosity. By way
of argument, he quoted the following passage from Gogol's *The Wedding:*

> KOTCHKARYOFF: But what is she doing now? Why, this door must lead to her
> bedroom. (He goes near the door.)
> FEKLA (a woman): You impudent fellow! You are told that she is still dressing.
> KOTCHKARYOFF: What of it! What's the difference? I shall only peep in and
> nothing more. (He looks through the keyhole.)
> ZHEVAKIN: Let me look in, too, only one little peep.
> YAITCHNITSA: Let me look in, too.
> KOTCHKARYOFF: (Continuing to peep in) Why, there is nothing to be seen,
> gentlemen! You can't distinguish anything. Something white is appearing, a
> woman or a pillow. (All come to the door, however, and scramble to peep in.)

Meyerhold then wrote,

> We prefer the theatre with art but without a public to the theatre with a public
> but without art. For we know that after all had rushed to the door and tried to
> peep through the keyhole, Kotchkaryoff came with the news, "Sh! Somebody's
> coming!" and everyone jumped away from the door. To every shamelessness
> there is a limit.[6]

From Meyerhold's point of view, not only was such "morbid curiosity" in
bad taste but it was self-defeating as well. For him the theatre and life were
incompatible. Taking the point of view of such symbolists as Maeterlinck,
Bryusov, Blok, and Ivanov, he maintained that theatre was art, not life. As
such, it must not attempt to represent life by binding itself to natural laws but
must suggest, offer hints, evoke desired responses from the audience by following the laws peculiar to art alone. His goal was to stimulate the audience to

create in its own imagination emotional states or ideas or events only implied on the stage. To Stanislavsky nature was the greatest artist, and art's job, to a large extent, was to approximate it. To Meyerhold art created independently of nature, and though it could and did relate to life, it need not necessarily grow out of life.

Originally, then, Meyerhold's quarrel with Stanislavsky and realism was pretty much the orthodox symbolist revolt. Whereas the elements of a Stanislavsky *mise en scène* (based on an objective view of nature and of art as its imitation) were chosen for their ability to represent accurately on the stage the world of the play, the elements of the Meyerhold *mise en scène* (based on a subjective view of nature and of art as a symbol) were chosen for their ability to evoke in the mind of the viewer a vision of the world for which the play, to the director at least, was a symbol. Once he had analyzed a play and decided what to him was its "essence," Meyerhold then developed a production plan which sought to express that essence in decorations, costumes, lighting, the rhythm and pattern of stage movement, gesture, and speech. His image of the play was obviously primarily visual. "The word is but a design on the fabric of movement," he was fond of saying. And the actor was clearly considered not as an independently creative artist but rather as one of the elements in the moving picture—indeed all too often one of the least manageable of the elements. In order to make the actor blend into the picture better, Meyerhold moved the playing area far forward, to the very lip of the stage, backed by screens and drops painted by post-impressionist, cubist, and futurist artists. Against these canvases his actors moved like animated bas-reliefs. It was this point of view and these production techniques which characterized Meyerhold's work at the Komissarzhevskaya Theatre and so disillusioned the young Tairov that he quit after a year.

Later, in trying to find ways to create closer rapport between audience and actor, to better communicate his image-evoking symbols, Meyerhold eventually did away with representative scenery, the proscenium, the darkened auditorium, and—reminiscent of Reinhardt—developed a sort of temple of communal creation, with ramps running over and through the audience, stage machinery and lighting apparatus in full view, and actors mingling with spectators. From this he moved on to the use of various techniques from the more presentational theatres of antiquity, and eventually developed a purely presentational style similar to the commedia dell'arte and the seventeenth- and eighteenth-century Chinese and Japanese theatres. The theatre of the mask, of the grotesque, of frank theatricality became his medium. The actor exercised his art as an intermediary agent, "presenting" the play to the audience, which was to appreciate first the actor as a performer and then through him the play, almost as an excuse for his performance.

The logical end of such a path was to liberate the theatre from the playwright and allow the actor free rein for his creativity. Meyerhold tended more and more to look upon the playscript as so much raw material to do with as he wished, but he never turned the creative responsibility in his theatre over to the actor. It was he, Meyerhold, as a kind of super-actor, who invented each role and then molded each member of his company into the image of a given role as he, Meyerhold, saw it. Thus, no sooner was the actor freed from the chains of verisimilitude but—in Meyerhold's theatre at least—he was bound by the even more demanding fetters of the director's "theatrical" production plan. At the same time, Meyerhold gave up his attempts to fuse the actor and spectator into a communal creative ritual and admitted the fundamental division between actor and spectator as one of the distinctive characteristics of theatre art.

5

By the time Tairov was emerging as a theatrical power in Moscow, then, Stanislavsky was still the champion of representational theatre, while Meyerhold stood opposed with a modernized version of the presentational. Stanislavsky's players ignored the audience, Meyerhold's never for a moment forgot it. With respect to the place of the actor in the creative activity of play production, there was also a sharp difference. Under the Stanislavsky system, ideally, the individual role was created by the actor himself, stimulated and aided by the director, who acted as teacher and mirror and who "created" the play as a whole by integrating the creative activities of the actors, designers, and technicians in the work of faithfully bringing to life the author's world. Ideally, each bit of business stemmed originally from the sincere emotional reactions of the actor, living over his part in the situations given in the play. The director suggested and selected but also tried to help the actor to create as much as possible, rather than imposing on him his own ideas. All the actor's training was designed to help him become a more dependable creator in his own right, re-creating his role at each performance.

In Meyerhold's theatre, actors were apparently treated simply as one of the media of the director's art—clay to be molded into forms congruent with the overall design. The actor was trained to sharpen his senses, his physical reflexes. He was trained to be physically hypersensitive to his surroundings, to physical stimulation. He was trained to submit his body completely to the control of his will so that with the least effort and utmost accuracy he could carry out at the request of the director actions dictated not because they grew out of the character but because they fit into the directoral design. In the Stanislavsky theatre, every actor was a creator in his own right. In the Meyerhold theatre, there was only one creator—the director. The actors were the focus of the *mise en scène,* but they did not share in its creation.

After the revolution Meyerhold developed his ideas on acting into a system of actor training which he called bio-mechanics. The theory behind bio-mechanics was based on a world view which admitted chemistry, biology, and physics, but not that mysterious "soul" which was made so much of in Stanislavsky's system. The basic assumption of bio-mechanics was that man is a highly developed animal, different in degree from other animals but not in kind. Man's contact with the world outside himself was thought to be maintained through the "elaborate mechanism" of the nervous system, which "reacts automatically to external influences." Man's so-called "soul" was taken to be merely "the aggregation of these impressions of the nervous system, just as the feeling of pain . . . is the result perhaps of pricking the finger."[7]

It logically followed that dramatic training really need be nothing more, basically, than a course in physical culture. The actor under Meyerhold's system was trained not to "feel" the life around him but to see it and touch it. Instead of training his "soul" by seeking out emotional experiences, he trained his reflexes, sharpened his physical perceptions by physical exercise. Anyone who had the "necessary ability for reflex stimulus" could become an actor.

Of course the political implications of this theory were obvious. The "priesthood" of acting was overthrown. The proletariat at long last was admitted not only into the theatre but onto the stage. Anyone with suitable reflexes could act. And as a matter of fact anyone *did* act, in Meyerhold's Theatres of October, all over Russia—in factories, in clubs, in villages. Peasants, workers, clerks, and soldiers clambered onto the stage and acted out party slogans, propaganda "pot-boilers," and local originals. But the major motive behind the invention of bio-mechanics was not political; it was artistic. It stemmed from Meyerhold's violent revolt against a theatre which was smothered in talk and psychologizing and starved for physical action, from his desire to educate for the Russian stage a generation of tempestuous, laughing, dancing, tumbling, *free-playing* comedians in the tradition of commedia dell'arte—men

who could supplement language with the pantomime of their expertly controlled bodies. It stemmed from his dream of bringing back to the Russian
theatre gesture, movement, physical life, and freeing it from the restrictions of
"inner realism" and its slavery to the word.

There was of course considerable, perfectly tenable ground between
Stanislavsky and Meyerhold, and it was far from being a no man's land. It was
very much occupied indeed, by directors such as Komissarzhevsky, Evreinov,
Vakhtangov, and Tairov himself. These men were first of all highly talented
and thoroughly trained practical men of the theatre. They were also well-edu-
cated and articulate theorists. All of them in one way or another sought a
so-called "synthetic" theatre in which all the arts were thoroughly integrated
in order to produce a work of *theatrical art,* not just an imitation of phenome-
nal reality: Komissarzhevsky's philosophical theatre, Evreinov's monodrama,
Vakhtangov's fantastic realism, and Tairov's synthetic theatre, or as he later
called it, neo-realism. Not only did these men publish articles and books
expounding their ideas, but they founded theatres to put them into practice.
With the exception of the Vakhtangov theatre, which is still one of the leading
theatres in Moscow though Vakhtangov himself died in 1922, the longest-lived
of these enterprises was Tairov's Kamerny Theatre.

6

Alexander Tairov had left the theatre in 1912 because it seemed to him
that the naturalistic theatre was tongue-tied and hamstrung by virtue of its
slavish imitation of real life. Worse, it was actually the slave of two masters,
for it was tied helplessly to literature, devoted to the faithful scenic embodiment of a given piece of dramatic literature. He found nothing creative in such
imitation. The realistic theatre of Stanislavsky and others was all inconsequen-
tial talk in everyday language, morbid psychologizing, neurotic display of emotion without form.

On the other hand, the "conditional" or stylized theatre of Meyerhold
(in 1912, remember) had faults just as serious, so far as Tairov was concerned.
Form it did indeed have, but it was empty form. The actors were so many
puppets, capable of making pretty pictures but devoid of the capacity to infect
an audience with that living scenic emotion which is the core of the theatre.
To be sure, such a theatre had freed itself from servitude to the playwright,
but it had placed itself in the just as tyrannous hands of the painter.

Dissatisfied, therefore, with both the realistic and the stylized theatre,

Tairov founded his own theory of theatre on two premises. The first was that there are two kinds of truth—the truth of life and the truth of art. "Naturally they coincide here and there," Tairov explained, "but for the most part what is true in life is not true in art, and artistic truth rings false in life." His second premise was that artistic truth, on the stage, may be found not in empty forms, however pleasing to the eye, but only in forms which had grown out of genuine, creative, theatrical emotion, had been polished to express that emotion clearly and vividly, and then in performance had been once more saturated with it.

Although he did not express it in precisely these terms, it seems clear that Tairov recognized that theatrical art takes place neither solely on the stage, as was the premise of the realistic theatre, nor solely in the mind of the audience, as was the symbolist-oriented premise of the stylized theatre, but in the dynamic interaction between the audience and the stage, between the spectator and the perceived work of art. In order to successfully achieve such interaction, in order to accomplish the necessary affective communication, neither aesthetically pleasing empty forms nor moving but formless emotionalizing was fully competent. Only both together, form and emotion, "emotionally saturated form," could achieve fully this dynamic contact which was the secret of theatrical art.

This, then, was that synthesis which Tairov thought could lead the theatre out of the bog of realistic soul-searching, around the nettle trap of empty formalism, and onto the path toward a joyfully creative "true" art of the theatre.

One of Tairov's primary interests was the place of literature in the theatre, his conviction being, actually, that it had no place, that the theatre was an art to be valued in and of itself, and was not the purveyor of literary works through the mouths of actors. In this respect, Tairov's position was even more extreme than Meyerhold's. Meyerhold, in spite of his highhanded use of scripts, did maintain that the theatre grew out of literature and would always be in some way dependent on it. Tairov insisted that though he used literature now as raw material, ideally the theatre should create freely, spontaneously, independently—the theatrical collective making its own scenarios and the actors filling in dialogue extemporaneously, except for moments when the emotional content demanded poetic language, in which case, the poet, working along with the collective, would compose the required set speeches. He was convinced this could be done once one had a company of master-actors, who could take an idea, through collective improvisation work out a scenario, and then in improvisational performance similar to commedia dell'arte present a pure work of theatre art to the audience. Since this was as yet impractical, he condescended to work with written plays as well as short stories—Hoffmann's "Princess Brambilla," for instance—but used them only as raw material to feed the furnace of theatrical fantasy.

Like Meyerhold, Tairov demanded that the actor's art be conscious and that the audience's appreciation also be conscious. The audience knows that the scenic figure is not a real person but the construct of the actor, and it must be allowed to appreciate the artistry of the actor's work, as actor, even while at the same time suffering empathic pangs for the agonies of the figure. Thus acting should not be constrained to simulate naturalness. On the contrary, it should be aimed at creating a physical and vocal form which expresses rather than represents the essence of the figure and its emotional state at any given time.

The term "express" here is important. Art's task is not to represent the figure as it is in life, but rather to penetrate to the core of that character as a representative of man in a given situation and to express that essence in vivid, concentrated, unambiguous forms. From this point of view, of course, both the realistic and stylistic theatres were at fault. The former stifled the actor's creativity, robbing him of theatrically expressive speech and gesture in the pursuit of naturalness; the latter—through insisting on forms of expression which would conform to an already conceived *mise en scène,* worked out by the director and scene designer—imposed form on the actor from without, thus disabling him from filling the forms with real scenic emotion.

Like Meyerhold, Tairov gave primacy to the gesture over the word. But he accused Meyerhold of dealing with empty gestures, whereas he himself saturated gesture with emotion. Emotional gesture, emotional form, he said, is the secret to creativity in the theatre. He further insisted, in opposition he thought to Stanislavsky, that such emotion should come not from the emotion memory, from the experiential past of the actor himself, but from the stage life of the scenic figure the actor was creating. How that emotion was to be engendered, how that spontaneous act of creativity using the fantasy rather than emotion memory was to come about, he left veiled in mystery, insisting that if it were possible to explain it, it would no longer be an art.

Tairov also insisted that Meyerhold had made a puppet of the actor, while he worked in close cooperation with the actor as an independently creative artist; therefore, Tairov's final product was indeed the result of a cooperative creative endeavor. Reports by people who worked with him and observed his rehearsals, however, indicate that, as in Meyerhold's theatre, the dominating creator, indeed the dictator in his theatre (albeit a benevolent one), was Tairov himself; his actors obeyed his directions out of love perhaps rather than fear—unlike those of Meyerhold—but nevertheless spent a good deal more time doing what he told them than they did creating on their own. It is true, however, that whereas Meyerhold, the consummate actor himself, did a good deal of demonstrating which the actor was expected to copy, Tairov directed verbally, allowing the actor to find his own means, so far as possible, of carrying out the directions.

Whatever may have been his practice, Tairov insisted that the primary creator of the ideal theatre must be the actor—the master-actor, who could not only "act" but dance, sing, clown, juggle, and, in the tradition of commedia dell'arte, improvise dialogue as well as business, truly creating a new work of scenic art at each performance, with only a scenario as a base.

Having made the actor the center of theatre art, Tairov found it necessary to construct a "scenic atmosphere" which harmonized with the three-dimensional actor physically and which expressed in mass, line, and color the emotional content which the actor expressed through voice, movement, and gesture. Thus the set had to be three-dimensional. And of course the forms which made up this "atmosphere" need not represent anything ever before seen in nature. They needed only to express successfully the mood of the play. Tairov's comments in this regard sound reminiscent of Adolphe Appia and Gordon Craig.

7

Having mentioned Appia and Craig, I might here point out Tairov's relation to other notable contemporaries in Western Europe. His similarity to Jacques Copeau, for instance, is particularly striking. In 1913 Copeau, too, withdrew from the commercial theatre in revolt against the forms of naturalism and symbolism alike and organized his Vieux Colombier. He, too, felt that the art of the theatre was the art of the actor, not the playwright or the painter. He, too, founded a school of acting to train the master-actors which would be the core of his new theatre. In his staging he was careful to place his focus, as was Tairov, on the actor, not overpowering him with scenery and costumes but allowing him to stand out in sharp relief in a three-dimensional set of simple, formal design. Indeed, he was more true to his convictions in this respect than was Tairov. He cried for a bare trestle and no more. He was convinced that the future of the theatre did not at all lie in more complicated and perfect machines. Tairov, on the other hand, was filled with a vision of scenery, lighting, and costume which would be extensions of the actor's will and would one day blend with him in one supreme gesture at the point where the actor alone would reach his limit. He made use of the most notable Russian designers of the new school—Vesnin, Goncharova, Yakovlev, Ekster—and was prevented from using Salzmann's new lighting system only by inability to purchase necessary equipment because of the war.

Another Western contemporary whose concept of stage space particularly was similar to Tairov's was Leopold Jessner. Like Tairov, Jessner wished to give to stage movement vertical as well as horizontal dimension by using steps and platforms. Tairov's arrangement of levels in his description of an ideal ballet setting or in his setting for *Famira Kifared* were quite similar to the famous Jessner Treppen. Tairov's rhythmic orchestration of the movements of actors about these forms was also similar to Jessner's, as was his use of ambient light which filled the remaining space with emotion-evoking color and movement. Jessner's effort to express relationships by means of gesture rather than words was also similar to Tairov's. There was also similarity in the symbolic use of spatial relationships and color in costuming. However, whereas Jessner was concerned with "intensity" of expression—sometimes, according to his critics, at the expense of beauty—Tairov was always concerned with making his emotionally saturated forms also beautiful. Indeed, his critics often accused him of an over-concern with beauty to the neglect of intellectual content. Jessner and Tairov did agree, however, in their demands that the setting, whatever its expressive qualities visually, had also to be functional; that is to say, the structure of the acting platform on which the actor trod determined in considerable degree the rhythm of his movements.

Which brings us to the distinctive feature of the Kamerny Theatre and the creative key to every production directed by Tairov—rhythm. It is understandable in light of his idealist aesthetics that Tairov should recognize music as the most independent and most pure of all the arts. And it of course follows that he should, therefore, seek to make his productions approach music so far as possible. Thus the dialogue of his productions was not so much spoken as intoned, not quite in recitative, but in richly rhythmic and sustained tone, poetic utterance. His movement was not quite dance, but nevertheless choreographed, flowing, sustained, rhythmic, elevated, artistically designed movement. His sets were designed as "keyboards for the actor's playing." A musical score was composed for each production. Stanislavsky had banished the orchestra from the theatre. Tairov brought it back.

8

It should be clear by now that though at the outset of this essay Tairov was represented as occupying some part of the middle ground between Stanislavsky and Meyerhold, he is far closer to the latter. In his *Notes,* Tairov is hardly fair to Meyerhold. He criticizes the great theatricalist for making a "picturesque blemish" of the actor, when, in fact, by 1921 Meyerhold was just as convinced of the essentially dynamic nature of the theatre as was Tairov and was making the actor the sole bearer of theatrical art—at least in theory. In other ways, also, the two were similar. They both used the techniques of folk theatre and insisted on the relative independence of theatre from literature. They were similar in their emphasis on movement and gesture-pantomime as the basic medium of histrionic communication. They were alike in their insistence that the actor combine in one person the talents of acrobat, jongleur, clown, and songster—only the wide mastery of those physical and vocal techniques could result in the remarkable versatility of actors worthy of the name "master." Their interest in rhythm, in the musical content of the play, was also similar.

Nevertheless, there was an area of basic, indeed profound, disagreement. Tairov was concerned with beauty. His goal in mounting a play was to make it a thing of smooth, polished, refined, sensual beauty. Meyerhold was not concerned with such aestheticism. His methods were rough and bold. His *mises en scène,* full of machines and trapezes and acrobatics, were raucous and blatant. Meyerhold's theatre smacked of the circus, Tairov's of the ballet. The Bolshevik critics who called Tairov by comparison effete, steeped in petty bourgeois aestheticism, were, after all, not making things up. Compared to the roaring, husky, brawling theatre of Meyerhold during the early twenties he must indeed have seemed just that.

In spite of their apparent antipathy for each other, both Meyerhold and Tairov were at least agreed that the theatre as such was worth saving. In this respect one might consider them both representatives of the middle ground in the stratification of post-revolutionary tendencies. On the right were such theatres as the Moscow Art and the Mali, which stood for the preservation of traditional—basically illusionistic—theatre. On the left were the advocates of an art which should merge with life. The theatre was dead, they cried. Why continue working with a corpse? Find a new, more vital form. The latter group sounded very much like the current American champions for the theatre of happenings, cabaret theatre, psychedelic experiencings. Indeed, the attempts to "stage" productions of factory life in actual factories with the factory workers as participants, or the "mass-action" spectacles such as the First of May Festival of the Liberation of Labor, directed by Annenkov and Kugel, or the re-enactment of the taking of the Winter Palace, in which over six thousand persons took part, sound like current "organized" happenings, only on a grander scale and with clearly-defined political content and purpose. For all the differences there may be, the basic premise that the theatre as such is dead and now we must try, as Evreinov said, to "theatricalize life," is surely the same.

Meyerhold experimented with "communal" theatre and mass actions for a time. Tairov never did. But he was faced with his own dilemma. It is fascinating to follow Tairov's arguments in light of the current dilemma of the American theatre. He voices the same general objections to the realistic play and to "method" acting that we hear today. At the same time he warns against the overreaction of the stylized theatre, which sacrifices the actor to the decorative artist and fills the stage with empty forms, devoid of that emotional content which alone can give life and human pertinence to any work of theatre art. It is remarkable indeed how pertinent and timely the text of his *Notes* is after forty-eight years.

9

Tairov opened his Kamerny Theatre in 1914, and for six years, through war and revolution and famine, he struggled for the realization of his ideal "synthetic" theatre. By 1920 it seemed to him that he had accomplished the first step toward that realization. He had clarified his goals and he had found, after countless experiments, the path which would lead him to them. It was time, then, to consolidate his notes, organize the record of his achievements, clarify the lessons learned, and point out more clearly thereby his future route.

There were other reasons for the advisability of such a careful evaluation of the Kamerny's goals and methods, however. Tairov's theatre had been a source of considerable controversy even before the Revolution. Its anti-literary inclination, its concern with form and feeling at the expense, said its critics, of intellectual content, the importance Tairov gave to the bare body as a part of the rhythmic design of his productions—all these were bound to stimulate criticism. But after the Revolution the criticism became stronger and more official.

In 1917 Tairov wrote a pamphlet called *Proklamatsii Khudozhnika (Proclamations of an Artist)* in which he insisted upon art's independence of politics and declared that the current political events had nothing specifically to do with the Kamerny Theatre. Not that he was in any way opposed to the Revolution as such. On the contrary, he welcomed it. He saw in it the opportunity to break once and for all with the decaying traditions of a Philistine society and a marvelous stimulus to create new art forms. But his claim of strict independence for his theatre, his lack of concern, as an artist, with the class struggle as such was disquieting to those who were pledging their theatres as weapons in the class struggle and in the war against the ignorance and cultural deprivation of the masses.

Tairov followed this announcement by productions of Paul Claudel's "mystico-religious Catholic" plays *l'Echange (Exchange)* and *Tidings Brought to Mary* in 1918 and 1920, respectively. This was too much. The productions evoked vigorous protests from the Bolshevik critics. In spite of such protests, however, Lunacharsky, the minister of education, named the Kamerny one of the official state academic theatres, along with the Moscow Mali and the Moscow Art. But for the rest of his career, Tairov was under constant pressure to give up his formalist experiments and produce plays of approved ideological content and style more comprehensible to the masses. Much of what he produced and everything he wrote from this time on is colored by his constant struggle with the demands made upon his art by the Revolution. His theory of "neo-realism," elaborated in the mid-thirties, his reworking of it into "constructive-realism" in the mid-forties were, of course, composed with extra-artistic considerations in mind.

Unfortunately, Tairov simply was not a man of the masses. Walter Van Gyseghen described him in 1938 as "the complete cosmopolitan, . . . the essence of European taste and sophistication." Van Gyseghen added, "Berlin, Paris, New York—but particularly Paris—have left their indelible stamp upon him. His Russian courtesy and kindliness are expressed in a manner typically Parisian."[8] He had, after all, named his theatre *Kamerny* (chamber) precisely to signify that it intended its work for an audience of followers of sophisticated tastes and that it was firmly resolved "to work without depending on the general public, that Philistine firmly ensconced in the theatres." This last barb was aimed at the pre-revolutionary bourgeois audience, to be sure, but it applied, sadly enough, just as firmly to the post-revolutionary audiences of the proletariat. Nevertheless, from 1924 on, Tairov made valiant and apparently sincere efforts to reach a compromise between Bolshevik demands for a theatre which would appeal to the people and his own innate dedication to a theatre for the connoisseur.

Tairov's first production after returning from a tour of Western Europe in 1923 was *The Man Who was Thursday*, a dramatization of G. K. Chesterton's novel of political intrigue. In spite of the fact that it was not Soviet, Tairov had chosen the play in an effort to comply with demands that he select material more pertinent to Soviet life. The set for the production was constructivist, a technique which Meyerhold, then in high favor, was using as an expression of his concept of the stage as a tool for the actor-worker. Meyerhold's constructivist sets were purely functional. If they were designed to express anything, it was not the content of a given play but rather the Soviet glorification of the machine. Tairov's set for *The Man Who was Thursday*, however, was designed to express the mood and content (the atmosphere of the action) of this particular play. There was a difference, maybe not in outer form but in motivation for the use of this form, between Meyerhold and Tairov.

Criticism continued, and Tairov continued to seek a compromise which would satisfy the party and still not prostitute his artistic convictions. His productions of Soviet plays were not successful, and he turned again to the West, this time to Eugene O'Neill. In his productions of *The Hairy Ape, Desire Under the Elms,* and *All God's Chillun Got Wings,* he succeeded in dealing with material which, if not Soviet, at least represented (with the proper emphasis) violent condemnations of the bourgeois world. His productions, expressionistic as usual, but not so "dancy" and "singy" as *Salome* or *King Harlequin,* were landmarks in the staging of O'Neill.

In 1928 he produced Bulgakov's *The Purple Island,* a biting satire on party meddling in art. Tairov and Bulgakov were chastised and the production was removed from the repertoire. The next season Tairov produced Semyonov's *Natalya Tarpova,* which was also stricken from the repertoire because of anti-Soviet content. With Sophie Treadwell's *Machinal,* he again turned to the West for material. Indeed, from 1914 to 1934 Tairov was a cultural liaison between Russia and Western Europe. He introduced a large percentage of the Western repertoire to the Soviet Union, and his three tours to the West—1923, 1925, and 1930 (this latter taking him to Italy, Switzerland, Czechoslovakia, Uruguay, Argentina, and Brazil) made his Kamerny the most frequent visitor abroad among Soviet theatres of this period.

In 1933 Tairov seemed to strike the proper compromise with Vishnevski's *Optimistic Tragedy,* starring Alice Koonen as a female steel commissar. He was made a National Artist of the USSR in 1934. His success was short-lived, however. In 1936 he staged Bedy's *Bogatyrs (Heroes),* which satirized Russian epic heroes just at a time when the nation was making a concerted effort to increase national identification and pride in preparation for the war with Germany, which seemed to be imminent.

Tairov was chastised and the Kamerny placed in the hands of a committee.[9] He resumed control of the theatre in 1939, but it was clear that he either would not or could not conform consistently to the Party's wishes. The Kamerny continued to produce through the war, relocated first in Barnaul, in western Siberia, then Balkash, and finally in Irkutsk. In 1945 Tairov received the Order of Lenin. After the war the Kamerny returned to Moscow, but it had deteriorated badly. Under the pressures of "Zhdanovism" in 1946 Tairov made one final attempt to reconcile his artistic inclinations with the Party line. He failed, and in 1950 the theatre was closed. Tairov died the same year.

10

The Kamerny was one of the great theatres of the twentieth century, and Alexander Tairov was one of the great directors. He never mounted more than four new productions a year, and more than once chose to mount only one. The shows he did mount were meticulously designed and rehearsed. The technical perfection and polish of his productions was on a par with that of the Moscow Art Theatre and usually far outshone that of Meyerhold, whose productions, imaginative though they were, were too often "diamonds in the rough." The Kamerny productions of *Shakuntala, Salome, Adrienne Lecouvreur, Phaedra, Princess Brambilla, Famira Kifared, Giroflé-Girofla, Storm, The Hairy Ape, Desire Under the Elms, All God's Chillun Got Wings,* Shaw's *St. Joan,* Hasenclever's *Antigone,* and *Optimistic Tragedy* were landmarks in the history of theatre practice in the twentieth century.

It was Tairov's tragedy that his whole view of the theatre was aesthetic, not social, at a time when the concern of his society was just the reverse. He was a theatre artist of great talent, capable of creating on the stage organically unified forms which pleased the eye and ear and which expressed perfectly the emotion with which they were saturated. But their goal was not to enlighten the audience, any more than such could be the goal of a symphony. Their goal was to move and please. Such "formalism," of course, could not be condoned indefinitely in a society in which all the tools of enlightenment—the theatre numbered among them—were directed to the task of educating the masses to an awareness of the class struggle, illustrating the evils of bourgeois society, and bolstering enthusiasm for the building of socialism. From the mid-twenties on, Tairov's public utterances were those of a man essentially alienated from his society, struggling desperately to come to terms with it.

The present work, then, is to be regarded not as Tairov's last word on the subject of theatrical production, but his first. It is a fervent report on the first six years of his great experiment—to create a new theatre, to practice a self-contained art, independent of both literature and painting, and free of political tendency. He had as yet no political axe to grind. There were pressures on him from 1914 to 1921, but these were not political. He was free to do what he pleased in the first years of the Revolution, and he did just that.

Since both the man and his work were of such stature, the present text is one of the major documents in the history of modern theatre. Since, further, Tairov was seeking in his work a way out of a dilemma very like the one in which the American theatre currently finds itself, *Notes of a Director* has for us not only an historical but an immediate and practical pertinence.

WILLIAM KUHLKE

1.

Pro Domo Sua

I have intended several times to put my notes in order, but until now the active construction of a theatre has left me no time for the task. I am now making use of the first opportunity offered me to organize my notes and, having in this way reviewed once more the work already completed, to feel out more clearly and accurately our future route.

I warn you in advance: Do not expect from me either philosophical justifications or scientific generalizations. I am neither a philosopher nor a scientist. I am a director; I am the molder and builder of a theatre, and of all the sciences only one excites me—one which at present does not really exist—the "science" of our art. Furthermore, the secrets of this science are revealed not by means of the impartial scalpel of the scientist nor through the harsh lens of criticism but rather through the magic spectacles of Celionati, for which, as you know, one needs an especially long nose.

Neither am I a writer. Often I will not have the words to formulate a given principle clearly, but those who truly love the theatre and its wonderful art will be able to discern even under the pallid cover of my words the idea which is seeking expression—an idea born of vital and creative work *in* the theatre rather than a theoretical and critical view of it from outside.

To these lovers of the theatre I dedicate my book.

Above all I dedicate it to my brothers in arms and my students—to their tempestuous youth, to their fiery hearts, to their steadfast will to professional excellence. I dedicate it also to all those who are young and strong, whose flaming souls throb with the vision of a theatre—now at last being realized—which affirms an art of its own and a craft answerable to its own set of values.

I am not trying here to present universal and eternally valid formulas. I am trying only to put into words ideas which have crystallized in active, sound work in the theatre. Furthermore, I do not guarantee that future work will not recast in its fire that which has already been forged or that it will not add to our crystals new and unexpected facets.

Of one thing only am I positive: *The road to the theatre of our hopes lies through the complete overthrow of dilettantism and the utmost affirmation of professional excellence.*

To encourage the "faithful" making their way along this difficult path and to turn back the dilettantes, the unbelievers—that is the purpose of these notes.

In 1912, after a long period of vacillation and doubt, I decided at last to give up the theatre. I waited out the end of the season with difficulty, left St. Petersburg, and devoted myself to completely different work. It seemed to me that living in the provinces, in an atmosphere completely alien to the theatre, would help me to carry out my decision to leave the stage forever.

And I had to leave. The contemporary theatre no longer gave me joy or inspired me to work. On the contrary, with every day, with every production, the doubts festering within me grew, and at times it seemed to me that not just our theatre but theatre in general had lost the secret of its former charms, and now, enfeebled, was being drawn inevitably toward catastrophe. I thought about Duse, the beautiful Eleonora Duse, and her tragic break with the theatre; I remembered how only death prevented Komissarzhevskaya's intended resignation;[1] I was haunted by the disappointments of Gordon Craig and his exasperated apotheosis of the marionette. And over all, in triumphant stupidity, hovered the professorial cap of Eichenwald with his article "The Death of the Theatre."[2]

I knew of course that Eichenwald was wrong, that the theatre does not depend organically on literature and that its mission does not consist simply of the transmission of the playwright's work. To the "glosses" of Meyerhold I might add the whole epoch of Roman pantomime, when there were no authors or their plays, and nevertheless the theatre so charmed the spectator with its self-contained art that even the omnipotent Caesars envied the monuments with which the Romans honored their favorite mimes. I might remind the reader also of the brilliant revival of the commedia dell'arte, when Gozzi and Sacchi reopened the theatre of San Samuele, and the bells of Harlequin once more attracted crowds of Venetians and with their sparkling improvisations shattered the deceptive solidity of the success of Goldoni and his written plays.

I could cite many still more brilliant pages from the theatre's past as evidence that the art of the theatre and the actor is primary, and that Melpomene is far from being just a handmaiden among the muses.

And all this would still be only words, words, and more words, because the life of the theatre today not only does not corroborate them, it refutes them. Joy and youth have renounced the theatre, because, instead of wonderful flights into the fantastic region of the impossible, it struggles weakly in the snares of naturalistic banality or, wingless, drags itself about among the anemic, decadent conventions of formalism. And if Eichenwald was wrong with respect to the theatre as a whole, in its past and future, with respect to the contemporary theatre his words were substantially correct. For once the theatre ceases to be theatre, once it ceases to gladden and move the spectator with its own, self-contained, purely theatrical art and becomes only a transmitter of literature, then is it not really simpler and pleasanter to sit with the book in the comfortable quiet of one's study and there, without the troublesome glare of the footlights and the obtrusive interpretation of the actor, quietly read it? And could we ourselves—not critics, not philosophers, not professors, but actual theatre workers—sense the putrid smell of decay in our home and not abandon it?

How did it happen? What happened that the theatre, the beautiful theatre, conceived of Krishna and Dionysos, should change, as Sologub has said, into a cozy tomb for rabbits, and that the actor, the once proud mime, the bell-tinkling Harlequin, king of cloak and sword, should become a phonograph record, obediently repeating after the entrepreneur the words and "ideas" of Messrs. Artsybashev, Surguchev, and other "brother-writers"? 3

What has happened is that the theatre has lost the chief thing which distinguishes it from all other arts, which gives it its own peculiar joy. The theatre has lost the art and mastery of the actor. Need I say that in the theatre the chief thing is the actor, that in the history of the theatre there have been long periods when he existed without plays, when he managed without any kind of decoration, but that there has never been a single moment when there could be theatre without the actor! Need I recall Aristotle's definition, that the theatre is "the imitation of a single, important, self-contained *action*"—*action*, which of course is unthinkable without *one who acts*, i.e., without an actor.

Such being the case, since the essence of theatre is in the actor, then undoubtedly the development and state of the theatre at any given moment are directly dependent upon the development and state of the actor's art, and the

periods of rise and development of the theatre inevitably coincide with periods of the development of acting mastery, the periods of decline and crisis
with the periods of its decline. And that long crisis through which the contemporary theatre has suffered and which in the beginning of the twentieth century Gordon Craig tried to break through—along with Georg Fuchs (in his
book with the undeserved title *Revolution of the Theatre*) and here in Russia,
Meyerhold, Evreinov, and others—that crisis was in essence the inevitable and
logical result of a terrifying decline in acting mastery. And the dominance of
literature in the naturalistic theatre and the dominance of painting in the theatre of style stem from one and the same cause, from the actor's loss of his
own craftsmanship. For the actor devoid of his craft loses his power over the
spectator, and losing it he is powerless to fix the spectator's attention on himself. He then falls under the influence of the merely attendant elements of the
theatre, which focus the dominant interest of the spectator on themselves,
using the actor only as an unavoidable cover, without which even the blind
could see that the emperor is naked—that in fact there is no more theatre.

The emperor is naked; there is no theatre! With this grim conviction I left
the theatre.

A year passed. In August of 1913 I arrived in Moscow determined not to
get involved again with the theatre. I had made this decision without the
least hesitation because I considered myself "cured" once and for all. And
besides, not one of the existing theatres had any attraction for me, and the
thought of working in any of them did not in the least excite me.

But after several days had passed I began to feel that I was losing that
acquired tranquillity of which I was so proud. Every day the morning papers
brought new and sensational information about the "Free Theatre" which was
being organized:[4]

A theatre of all kinds of scenic art.
Monakhov, Chaliapin, Davidov, Koonen, Andreeva, Baltrushaytis, Duse, Sarah
Bernhardt, Salvini have been invited.[5]
Preparatory work is in full swing—millions are being spent on all kinds of experi-
ments.
The services of Reinhardt, Georg Fuchs, Gordon Craig . . . the Pope are being
enlisted for separate productions.
In the repertoire are drama, comedy, operetta, pantomime . . .

and on and on.

And among all these pieces of information, whimsically interlacing and tangling them, floated the strange, almost fantastic figure of Mardzhanov. He was a man who undoubtedly existed in several incarnations, for according to the newspapers he was working on *The Beautiful Elena* in Moscow, negotiating with Varlamov in St. Petersburg and Craig in Florence, watching *Yellow Jacket* in China, recruiting an orchestra in Prague, making arrangements for guest appearances abroad in London, and buying oxen in Sarochintsy for *The Sarochintsy Fair*—all at the same time. [6]

Several more days passed, and I met Mardzhanov. This man truly felt himself to be the "collector" of theatrical Russia. His troupe was already so large that the pit of the Hermitage Theatre could not accommodate it. For every production he had two directors and two candidates besides. And still he invited me as well to join the Free Theatre.

What should I do? Yes, I had renounced the theatre, but only because the contemporary theatre did not satisfy me. But a *new* theatre, a theatre in which one may attempt to find a way out of the agonizing impasse, one which wants to travel unbeaten paths, a theatre inspired by such a burning enthusiast as Mardzhanov. . . . Could I possibly resist for long? And when Mardzhanov offered me the production of a *pantomime,* something I had long dreamed about, the question was decided at once, and the piano score of *The Veil of Pierrette* soon was in my hands. [7]

I began work on *The Veil of Pierrette.* As I sat in the parterre, listening to the orchestra, the imperishable forms of Pierrot, Columbine, and Harlequin rose up within me to meet the melodies of Donani. Here Columbine and Pierrot entwined in tragic embrace; now the wedding candles of Death were burning; here, in the "Danse Macabre," Harlequin gyrated to the strains of the polka; finally, unconscious, the dying Columbine fell at the feet of the dead Pierrot.

How to translate all this into reality? How to transfer onto the stage all these flickering forms, these agitating harmonies, these enthralling rhythms? How to stage the pantomime?

Pantomime!

Was it not the progenitor of theatre during the time of Dionysos and in the cult of Krishna? Did it not attract avid crowds to the Roman amphitheatre? Did it not always rise up on the centuries-old path of the theatre as an invariable sign of its impending renaissance? Once more I felt the old excitement of the theatre, and together with the small group working with me I began seeking a way to bring the pantomime to life on the stage.

But upon what could we base our work? Where could we find a starting point for it? The pantomime, as a special form of theatrical art, had long ago disappeared from the stage. The ballet had gone over exclusively to dance, and circus pantomime had fallen into decay and was based on empty and uninteresting illustrative gesture. I did not think we should reconstruct the pantomime of the distant past. I did not have the spirit of an antiquarian, and I never thought it possible to feel in the theatre of antiquity the heartbeat of authentic contemporary theatre.

Obviously, then, I could not find a basis for our production in works on pantomime. One thing was left: to examine once more the path followed by the theatre over the last few decades, noting everything false and obsolete, and attempt to find that which was genuine and unchanging, and from there set out on our own unfamiliar and difficult path.

First, then, what about the naturalistic theatre with its servile worship of verisimilitude, its invariable urge to make "live pigs squeal"? Do you know the old Aesop fable which Coquelin tells as though it really happened? Once at a fair a minstrel began imitating the squeal of a pig. He did it so skillfully that everyone was amazed and began to applaud loudly. Whereupon a peasant bet that he could squeal just as well as the minstrel. He hid a live pig under his clothes and began to pinch it. Naturally the pig squealed. Nevertheless the peasant was hissed off the stage. "What can you do?" says Coquelin. "The pig squealed well enough to be sure, but without art."

Yes, there is nothing you can do about it, for there are two kinds of truth —the truth of life and the truth of art. Naturally they coincide here and there, but for the most part what is true in life is not true in art, and artistic truth rings false in life.

The naturalistic theatre either overlooked this simple truth or consciously rejected it. Hence its eagerness that both the actor and the audience forget about the theatre, that they feel just as though the drama or comedy being acted out on the stage were taking place in real life. Hence the demand that the actor be as it were a copy of a man taken from life—"artless"—that he move, speak, in general be so "natural" that the spectator has no doubt that before him is the actual Ivan Ivanovich and not actor X, the real Ekaterina Ivanovna and not actress Y. Hence the desire to create a set which completes the fraud, hence the odor of sauerkraut soup and the kitchen issuing from the depths of a stage upon which an entire house has been erected, etc., etc.

I remember my own sojourn with the Mobile Theatre, where I worked two years (1907-1908) as an actor and director.* The Mobile Theatre, especially in its early productions, had still not outgrown naturalistic illusions, so that in the play *Blessed Are Those Who Hunger* they built almost an entire house on stage from real logs just as stout as those used for peasant huts in villages (the action took place in the home of a country doctor). The theatre was mobile, and all these logs were carted from St. Petersburg to Kharkov, from Kharkov to Vyatka, etc.—all so that the walls, God help us, might not shake when the actors touched them and reveal to the audience the terrible secret that there was scenery on the stage. A lamp hung from the ceiling. It really burned and, naturally, flickered every time the door was opened. This signified that wind had burst into the room. But how was it that this wind left the tablecloth, the actors' hair and everything else in the room untouched? Since willy-nilly we could not counterfeit life completely, was it worth carting these logs from city to city?

I could cite a mass of similar examples from personal experience, but surely it is not necessary to resurrect all the contrivances of the naturalistic theatre and recall how mercilessly life itself destroys all its illusions, created with such difficulty. Thumb through Fuchs' book or the articles of Meyerhold, and the artistic bankruptcy of the naturalistic theatre will reveal itself to you in full measure.[8]

Another question interested me, a much more important and significant one and one which Fuchs and Meyerhold barely touched. This question concerned *the actor's creativity and the approach routes to it,* and it had to be answered before we could even begin work on the pantomime.

The chief demand which the naturalistic theatre made upon the actor was that his emotional experiences on stage be truthful, sincere, and natural. To achieve this he had first of all to forget that he was on a stage; he had to forget that he was an actor. Relying on "emotion memory," he was supposed to be so convincing that the spectator never doubted even for a moment that before him stood not an actor but an honest-to-goodness, ordinary person, taken right out of life, with his strengths and weaknesses, his suffering and happiness, tears and smiles, customs and habits. In order to achieve this goal the actor

*I staged there Shakespeare's *Hamlet* and *Eros and Psyche* by Zhulavsky. [The Mobile Theatre (Peredvizhnoi teatr) was founded in St. Petersburg in 1903 by P. P. Gaideburov and N. F. Skarskaya. It was very popular during the early years of the Soviet regime, finally closing in 1928. — Translator.]

had to be an alert observer of life; he had to go about as if with a pocket Kodak in his eyes and soul, so that afterwards, having experienced emotionally everything that had been observed, he could transfer it from life to the stage. It had to seem to the spectator as though real life were passing in front of him. Therefore the spiritual vibrations of the actor on the stage had to throb in unison with those of life; his voice had to be muffled, his speech simplified, his gesture restrained. In this way the actor was deprived of all the modes of expression, the only means by which he could reveal his art. He purposely changed from an actor into a sweet, sensitive person, not a bad psychologist and without fail a neurasthenic (remember, it was the naturalistic theatre which introduced this new and fascinating line of business)—a person who sincerely empathized with his fellow man, but who was incapable of creating theatre.

The actor, that is the craftsman who is master of his art, was in fact not needed by such a theatre. "Acting," and "actor" became almost derogatory words. A sweet, pathetic Russian intellectual rushed onto the stage and began publicly to turn his soul inside out. And since this was his primordial calling, things went very well, and the naturalistic theatre began to achieve tremendous successes.

In its efforts to transfer life onto the stage, the naturalistic theatre went so far as to invite a real choir boy to play the role of the choir boy in Gorky's *Petty Bourgeois*. One could go no further than that. Verisimilitude had triumphed, and the disgraced actor fled from the theatre. But along with him went the very essence of theatre, its art. And the theatre, unable to attract an audience by means of its own, self-contained art, little by little either turned into an experimental institute for psychopathology or became a popular guide to the history of Russian and foreign literature.

What could one take from such a theatre for work on a pantomime, where one cannot take cover behind the author's "idea," where one cannot fill the spectator with floods of the author's words, where the art of the actor is obliged to reveal itself in its essential form? According to the apt description of Yu. Slonimskaya, [9] the naturalistic theatre had been reduced to little more than "tongue-tied" gesture. Was it possible that this so-called "character gesture," this shallow, slovenly, tongue-tied gesture which expressed nothing could serve as a basis for the pantomime? Of course not.

Perhaps then "perezhivanie" would yield the sought-for key to our work. [10] To be sure, "perezhivanie" is a necessary step in every creative process, but it alone is not enough to create a work of any art, including the theatrical. Undoubtedly every artist, whether he be a painter, sculptor, musician, poet, or actor, must first "experience emotionally" the work of art which he intends to create. And only after having thus experienced it in his creative soul may he impart to it externally visible features, cast it in that form which is peculiar to it. But on the other hand, no creative idea, however thoroughly "experienced," may be in itself a work of art so long as it has not been molded into a visible form. For form is the sole means through which one's creativity may be perceived by others. Until the process of design has taken place, one may not produce a work of art. The naturalistic theatre suffers from a dysentery of formlessness.

Having concentrated exclusively on emotional experience, having deprived the actor of all his means of expression, having subordinated his creativity to truth to life with all its fortuitous circumstances, the naturalistic theatre had annihilated scenic form, which has its own laws not in the least dictated by life. Therefore, the naturalistic theatre was in essence not authentic theatre and never produced a finished work of scenic art. Now and then its performances did succeed in creating an impression of a designed stage production. For when Ivan Ivanovich was obliged to be Ivan Ivanovich on the stage as well, and Ekaterina Ivanovna to be Ekaterina Ivanovna, sometimes the very formlessness of the production, expressing and as it were embodying the formlessness of life, was taken mistakenly for self-contained scenic form. Is this not the clue to the naturalistic theatre's success with contemporary plays about everyday life and its almost invariable failure with other kinds of production?

And so, admitting the necessity of emotional experience (albeit of a different kind than that cultivated in the naturalistic theatre) in every creative process, including the scenic, and particularly in the creation of a pantomime, we had to find a form into which this "perezhivanie" might be cast. Undoubtedly the form of the pantomime is *gesture,* taken in its broadest sense. But what kind of gesture? Certainly not illustrative, and certainly not the life-like, "tongue-tied" gesture of naturalism. But what kind? Perhaps the conventional gesture of the stylized theatre.[11] Indeed, perhaps everything we need is to be found in just this kind of theatre, with its tireless search for form. After all, we too are striving after scenic form.

I remember how as young people in love with the theatre we avidly seized upon any information about the revolt against naturalism, with what excitement and hope we followed the vicissitudes of the battles which erupted, how joyfully we greeted the birth of the theatre of style. It seemed to carry within it that truth after which our spirits so hungered. It seemed predestined to return to the theatre its primordial strength. How cruelly disappointed we were when we realized from the experience of the pioneers of this theatre and from our own work that we had again arrived at a dead end—a different one, but just as agonizing and hopeless as the naturalistic theatre.

Only now, after many years have passed, do we understand that it could not have been otherwise. Thesis always gives birth to antithesis, and only then can the final process of synthesis take place. In the history of contemporary theatre the naturalistic theatre was the thesis, the antithesis of which had of necessity to be the stylized theatre. The time was not yet ripe for the synthesis.

One might have defined the line of the stylized theatre in three words: "On the contrary."

"Everything as in life," said the naturalistic theatre.

"Everything different from life," proclaimed the theatre of style.

"The spectator must forget that there is a stage before him."

"The spectator must never for a moment forget that he is in a theatre."

"The actor must feel just as he would in real life."

"The actor must remember every second that he is on a stage not in the street."

"The actor must truly experience everything."

"The actor ought not experience anything emotionally," etc., etc., etc.

I remember well the first public experiments and productions of the theatre of style at Vera Komissarzhevskaya's theatre in St. Petersburg in 1905-1906.* I remember also the rehearsals and the production work, which I, a young actor in this theatre, followed with eager attention. The three-dimensional sets which so enraged us with all their tasteless, life-like detail were destroyed. The real-life coats which so burdened the actors' shoulders were thrown away. Under the leadership of Sapunov and Sudeikin, [12] onto the stage came artists who had longed for great canvases and who responded happily to Meyerhold's call for joint endeavor.

"They came; they saw; they conquered."

Indeed, they conquered without effort. And if the naturalistic theatre

*The Moscow Theatre-Studio was not open to the public. [Tairov is referring here to the "theatre-studio" of the Moscow Art Theatre, which was organized by Stanislavsky in 1905, with Meyerhold as its director, for the purpose of seeking new and non-realistic forms of theatrical production.—Translator.]

turned out in the end to be a prisoner of literature, the stylized theatre almost from its first steps was the prisoner of painting. The entire stage, the whole task of organizing a production came to be looked at from the point of view of "beauty." But not the beauty of the actor's material, rather the beauty of the overall plan of decoration and the vision of the artist, in which the actor participated only as a necessary "picturesque blemish."

> The clumsy conglomeration on the stages of the naturalistic theatre was replaced in the New Theatre by the demand for *strict subordination* to rhythmic movement in line and to musical harmony among the picturesque blemishes.*

The result of such construction was that the actor was tolerated by the artist only so long as he remained a picturesque blemish, forgetting about the nature of his art, about action and the movement connected with it. For once he moved, the actor unavoidably shifted the "picturesque blemishes" and, naturally, spoiled the artist's picture. Hence the notorious striving of the stylized theatre for "statuesqueness." Hence not just economy but a stinginess, a poverty of gesture.

A most curious phenomenon characterized the life of the stylized theatre, and one should not let it pass without mention. Very often at the opening of the curtain the auditorium resounded with applause, and almost always the audience fell silent thereafter until the end of the act or even the play. This happened because the opening picture really deserved applause. Everything in it was complete and harmonious. But once the first moment had passed and the actor began to move, the charm of the picture disappeared and the interest of the audience began to fade. For the actor himself could not inspire such interest, and without it there can in essence be no theatre and, frankly, there was none.

I remember how the actor of the stylized theatre transformed himself. I remember how painstakingly the actors shucked "contemptible feelings" from their souls, how they strove—God save us—not to experience emotional suffering, anger, love, hate, or joy, but only coldly and calmly *to represent them. The representational method* became the chief dogma of their scenic faith and the main compass of their stage practice.

Thus to the first rehearsals (as it happened, for instance, during rehearsals for Maeterlinck's *Sister Beatrice*) Meyerhold would bring monographs on Memling, Botticelli, and other artists which corresponded to some incident or other

---

*Italics mine. See Meyerhold's article in Shipovnik's *Theatre Almanac.*

in the play, and the performers would take gestures from them. Often they copied entire groupings, portraying not only feelings but their outer manifestations, that is, form itself. It is no mere coincidence that in his article Meyerhold gratefully cites Valeri Briusov's review in *Vesy,* in which Briusov writes of the "theatre-studio" that "some groups seem to be Pompeiian frescoes *reproduced* in a living picture.*

Such a representational approach to the creation of form had, in essence, just as little value as the formlessness of the naturalistic theatre, which, so far as its external form was concerned, was also constructed according to a representational method (the reproduction of life). If we remember that, according to Meyerhold, "when we adhered to such a method we did not permit temperament to break through until we had mastered form,"** then the stylized theatre's *external* approach to the creation of scenic form becomes obvious.

And this had inevitably to lead to the mechanization of the actor, to the destruction of his creative ego. For if on the one hand "emotional experiencing" in itself, not cast in a corresponding form, does not constitute a work of scenic art, on the other, hollow form, not saturated with the corresponding emotions, cannot take the place of the living art of the actor.

Valeri Briusov, whom Meyerhold cites so often, states in his article, with inevitable logic, that for final victory it remains for the "stylized" theatre only "to replace the artists with dolls on strings and with gramophones inside. This would be consistent; it would be one of the possible solutions to the problem. There is no doubt that the path of the contemporary 'stylized' theatre leads straight to the theatre of marionettes."† It is undoubtedly so. Indeed, it could not be otherwise once the actor had been deprived of control over his own material, once he could no longer achieve a creative-emotional expression of form, once he was no longer the determining and decisive factor in the construction of scenic atmosphere.

Powerless to focus the attention of the spectator on himself, the actor had to yield to the newly powerful artist, who began to lord it over the stage. And of course the actor only got in the way of the artist, who had transferred to the stage all the methods of easel painting with its two-dimensional treatment. Above all the artist was disturbed by the actor's three-dimensional body. It

*Italics mine. [Valeri Briusov (1873-1924) was a leading symbolist poet. His review *The Scales* (Vesy) was the most important literary periodical of the time.—Translator.]
**The same article.
†Briusov, "Realism and Convention on the Stage."

was only natural, therefore, that "work on another piece *(The Death of Tintagiles)* produced a method of arranging stage groups *patterned after bas relief and frescoes*."* That is, the stylized theatre, in order to satisfy the artist, flattened out the three-dimensional actor so that he would not disturb the flat stage picture which was being created.

What was the actor to do?

Finally, wanting to move his canvas closer to the audience, the artist cut down the depth of the stage and pressed the actor up against the footlights, leaving him a playing area of no more than six or seven feet—just enough for a grave. Obviously there was only one way out: to lie down and die. Which in the end the actor of the stylized theatre solemnly did, and after him the theatre itself.

What a sad end our bright hopes had come to.

What could one take from the stylized theatre for work on the pantomime? Form? No, that was not the form we were striving for. Gesture? No, mechanized gesture had no place in our quest; it was not the goal toward which we were intuitively groping our way.

And so we began our work.

Guided only by *negative* principles—that our way was not the way of either the naturalistic or the stylized theatre—and having agreed only that we were going to seek a new, self-contained, scenic form and that in our search we would always proceed from the particular nature of the acting material, we took up our work.

We worked very hard, far removed from the "Sarochintsy Fair" of the Free Theatre. From time to time we called Mardzhanov to us in order to share some failure or a happy moment of discovery.

We groped our way along. But how fascinating was our ignorance, our child-like innocence, when we gave ourselves up for hours at a time to the music of Donani; in fantastic, limitless spaces the mute figure of Pierrot glided before us, and Pierrette, senseless, her wedding veil lost, was swept after him in a vortex of harmony. But Harlequin, in mighty swellings of brass which seemed to rage out over the whole world, as well as his guests, obsequious progeny of his power and fantasy—all suddenly died away when Columbine appeared again in the rising chords of the harp. The wild fury of the *Schnellpolka* crowned the treacherous revelry of Harlequin, and amid the quavering

*Meyerhold, *ibid.* Italics mine.

expirations of flutes, the light of reason flickered out in the exhausted body of Pierrette.

Yes, this was in an entirely different sphere, on a different plane than our everyday life. Here eternal figures were locked in combat; the primordial images of the human creature, having done away with the world of everyday, were in the throes of the last engagement, the struggle between love and death.

It was clear that we must discard the vulgar, chopped-beef scenario with its triviality, its pettiness, its dialogues—"Pierrette: Let us fly!" "Pierrot: But I have no money."—which led to uninteresting, illustrative gesture.

Only the age-old sketch of the final duel among Pierrot, Pierrette, and Harlequin should be left, and the action should be transferred to a plane of the most intense emotion. Then illustrative gestures, conventionalized informative actions, feelings, and words would not be needed. For in moments of maximum emotional strain, *silence* sets in. Think of the common phrases, "I have no words to express . . . " etc., etc. Consider the origin of *pauses* on the stage. Remember the brilliant stage direction of Pushkin, "The people remain silent." [13] No, the pantomime is not a presentation for the deaf and dumb, where gestures replace words. The pantomime is a production of such scope, such spiritual revelation that *words die,* and in their stead genuine scenic *action* is born—scenic action in its primary aspect, the form of which is saturated with intense creative *emotion,* seeking an outlet *in corresponding gesture.*

Emotional gesture—only it has the power to reveal the true art of theatre, the art of pantomime. Only it will give the key to the discovery of genuine form, form saturated with creative emotion—*emotional form.*

"Emotional gesture," "emotional form"—this is that *scenic synthesis* toward which we were gropingly moving in our work, without which there was no way out for the *contemporary theatre*—indeed for theatre generally.

Music! It was she, and the magic of her rhythms, which helped us to experience emotionally the delightful process of the birth of the scenic synthesis, to become aware of the first timid pulse of emotional form within us.

Our group experienced two moments of tremendous excitement. The first, when after three months of work we showed the results to the troupe of the Free Theatre. The second, soon after, when the first performance of *The Veil of Pierrette* took place. We knew that on both occasions distrust, skepticism, and prejudice awaited us. How happy we were when both the troupe and the audience turned out to be thrilled by the production, when yesterday's detractors (actors of the Free Theatre and others, including the Moscow Art Theatre) excitedly congratulated us, and Scriabin said that this production could induce him to write for the theatre. And this in spite of the fact that we ourselves admitted that we had accomplished only a very small part of what we were capable of.

Now, after an interval of six years, I see clearly what a significant influence both the naturalistic and the stylistic theatres had on our work, how many mistakes we made, and what a small part of the truth of the theatre our intuitive groping had managed to draw out. Apart from the vast amount of internal work, which itself required not months but years, we had further to master a new craft of acting. Only then would we be in a position actually to incarnate our feelings and visions. And our young actors— against a background of simple, uninteresting scenery in the modernistic style of the period,* deprived of the cover provided by words, still struggling with the principles of creative embodiment of emotional gesture (emotional form)—nevertheless joyfully moved the audience with their performance.

What enormous possibilities, what extraordinary wonders awaited the theatre there on the unknown heights of that imminent scenic synthesis. In spite of our lack of technical skill, in spite of the fact that we were still only timidly approaching a breakthrough to a new secret of theatre, the charm of our performance was so great that it infected even the most inveterate skeptics in the parterre.

A season passed.

Besides *The Veil of Pierrette* I managed to carry out several interesting experiments in connection with the production of *The Yellow Jacket.* Meanwhile, the Free Theatre, having burst over the dull, humdrum theatrical world like a brilliant firework, died.

The reasons for its fall, unfortunately, were contained in the very organization of the Free Theatre. People of too many different languages, artists of almost inimical trends, were gathered within its all-embracing walls. Thus when the patrons, apparently having been mistaken in their estimates of cost, withdrew support, the whole structure, this remarkable Tower of Babel which Mardzhanov had erected with such love, collapsed. And so the Free Theatre died.

---

*The model had been worked out before I joined the theatre.

In concluding my discussion of the Free Theatre, I must first clear up an old and obstinate misunderstanding. It has become very stylish of late to speak and write—whenever and wherever—about the so-called "synthetic theatre," injecting into this concept a completely false meaning. For some reason those theatres are called "synthetic" which present in turn now a drama, now an opera, now an operetta, now a ballet—theatres, that is, which join together *mechanically* various kinds of theatre art. In such theatres (for instance in the short-lived New Theatre of F. Komissarzhevsky) there are even separate troupes for drama, opera, ballet, etc.[14] To call such theatres synthetic is, of course, absurd.

A synthetic theatre is one which fuses *organically* the various scenic arts so that in a single performance all those elements which are now separated—dialogue, singing, dance, pantomime, even elements of the circus—are harmoniously combined to produce a single, *monolithic* theatrical work. Such a theatre by its very nature cannot tolerate separate actors of drama, ballet, opera, etc. It requires a new *master-actor,* who commands all the resources of his many-faceted art with equal ease.

For the information of all those recidivists who intentionally or unintentionally persist in misusing the long-suffering term "synthetic theatre," I count it only just to point out that from this point of view the first such theatre was the Free Theatre, which during the one season of its existence presented the opera *The Sarochintsy Fair,* the operetta *Beautiful Elena,* the pantomime *The Veil of Pierrette,* the drama *The Yellow Jacket,* and the melodrama *l'Arlesienne.* The first founder of such a theatre in our times was Mardzhanov.

So, the Free Theatre died. Nevertheless it was clear to me and to the small group of people united with me in art that the work we had begun must not stop, that the new modes of theatre which it had engendered must find some means of realization. We must continue our quest until at last, in the magic currents of the wondrous lake Urdar,[15] we saw the reflection of that truth which had drawn us on.

It was also clear that we could not work in any of the existing theatres.

We must have our own theatre.

Our own theatre!

Who can count the sleepless nights, the days full of hope and despair, the projects which unexpectedly proved completely impractical, the almost delirious constructions which like fantastic castles in the air rose and fell in the spring torpor of the indifferent city.

To build a theatre one needs a place, a troupe, and money. We had none of these. Nevertheless the Kamerny Theatre came into being.

How?

How is morning born?

How does spring arrive?

How is human creativity engendered?

The Kamerny Theatre was born in the same way, with all the incomprehensibility and all the elemental logicality of such an origin.

It *had* to be born. It was written in the book of theatrical fate.

Otherwise, how could it have happened that in all of great, muddled Moscow, house number twenty-three Tversky Boulevard should be discovered, in which the proprietors themselves had been thinking of building a theatre. How could it happen that the military, solidly billeted in the halls of the ancient residence, had just stayed out the last months of their contract. How could it have happened that we, having categorically refused patronage,* suddenly, in the last minute, having almost lost hope, found two shareholders and brought 10,000 rubles to the proprietors, signing an agreement with them for five years for a total of 175,000 rubles! How could it have happened that in the twentieth century, giving no kind of monetary guarantee, we nevertheless gathered about us the necessary group of young, talented actors, ready to work with us under any conditions. How could it have happened . . . .

But no. I cannot possibly list or explain all the "hows."

You want to know the story of the birth of the Kamerny Theatre? Read *A Thousand and One Nights.* Read the fantastic tales of Hoffmann. Thumb through the pages of Jules Verne, Main Read, and H. G. Wells. Then perhaps you will get some idea of how the Kamerny Theatre came into being, or, rather, how until the last moment we ourselves did not know whether it had actually been realized or whether it was only a delirium, a caprice of our theatrical imagination.

In the phantasmagoria surrounding the birth of the Kamerny Theatre the boundaries of the imagined and the real became so entangled—it happened often that the whole project seemed to have died and then in some unexpected fashion suddenly decked itself out again in flesh and blood—that when the first posters with the headline "Kamerny Theatre" at last appeared on the streets of Moscow, we asked passersby to read them to us aloud, so as to confirm indisputably that it was really true and not a mirage, not a figment of our fevered imaginations.

So, the Kamerny Theatre became a fact.

*The experience of the Free Theatre had taught us our lesson.

Why Kamerny? This question was put to us often both at the time of its origin and later. To me and my colleagues this name seemed quite clear and natural.

Nothing new in art ever finds immediate access to the artistic sensibilities of the general public. It was not for nothing that Oscar Wilde wrote that more than anything in the world the public fears innovations and in order to protect itself against them has constructed barricades of the classics and established its own cadre of critics. The example of the Free Theatre confirmed this.

We wanted to work without depending on the general public, that Philistine firmly ensconced in the theatres. We wanted to have a small chamber audience of *our own* spectators, dissatisfied, restless seekers such as we. We wanted to say straight off to the proliferating theatrical Philistine that we did not seek his friendship and did not want his after-dinner visits.

That is why we named our theatre Kamerny.

But of course we never for a moment intended that this name should restrict us or limit our creativity in any way. We aspired neither to chamber repertoire nor to chamber methods of production and performance. On the contrary, their very existence was alien to our intention and our quest.

Now the name has in large measure already lost its original meaning, but we preserve it as a man preserves the name he was given at birth.

We decided to open the theatre with *Shakuntala*.

We were attracted by the fine grandeur, power, and tenderness, enticed by the mystery of Kalidasa's remarkable creation. We were captivated by the possibility of being the first to make contact with the secrets and manners of Indian theatre.

Besides all this, tradition, which jealously guarded the approaches to every other classical work, did not lie in wait for us in this one; and it seemed to us that in it we could more easily free ourselves from the methods of the contemporary theatre because of the great gulf which separated it from the hoary days of Krishna.

And so we began to dream with enthusiasm of the work before us. But in so far as it fell to me, as director, to concretize these dreams, I began to feel that our intended work was as difficult as it was fascinating.

Anxiety over our first production overcame even the excitement of having my own theatre; and giving my closest co-workers a series of assignments concerning the theatre and its construction, I went abroad, so that forcibly removed from organizational problems I might concentrate exclusively on the production.

I stayed in Paris and London. Full of enthusiasm, I spent days at a time in the Indian rooms of the Musée Guimet, the British Museum, and a special Indian Museum, sketching and making notes of the various plans for our forthcoming production which arose in my imagination. But in spite of the colossal amount of invaluable material I uncovered, I was dissatisfied. I was irresistibly drawn back to Moscow, to the theatre, *to the stage*. Only there, I felt, in actual contact with the actors, could the production plan I saw in my mind's eye be developed and given final form.

External events also prompted me to hurry my departure. War unexpectedly became imminent, and only with great difficulty did I manage to get on the last train leaving Paris. It was literally a miracle that I made my way back to Moscow.

In Moscow a million misfortunes awaited me. Frightened by the war, the workers had fled to the country, and the construction of the theatre was bogged down in a half-completed and perilous state. The better part of the young men on whom I had placed such high hopes had been drafted. Alice Koonen, who was to play Shakuntala, was stranded abroad. The translation of the mystery had still not been sent from Paris where Konstantin Balmont was working on it. [16] There was not a cent in the box office, and on top of everything, war, war, war.

What was there to do?

Everyone assured me—and indeed I myself could see—that war upsets all plans, that the appearance of this *force-majeure* put an end to all obligations, that construction which had been started would remain unfinished, that to establish a theatre just as a war was beginning was impossible, that to continue to hope and work, insane.

Nevertheless I hoped and worked.

An agonizing month passed, during which at times I thought I would go mad. Meanwhile the hearty sound of resumed construction at last resounded through the building; and in a cramped little room, the only one where there was no construction work and where presently the public cloak room would be situated, we began strenuous, around-the-clock rehearsals for the production—in a translation by Balmont and with Alice Koonen in the role of Shakuntala.

For the Kamerny Theatre had to be born.

In staging *Shakuntala* I had to carry out a very large and complicated piece of work. The task of staging the mystery—perhaps too extraordinary, too monumental for our theatre—often overwhelmed me with its magnitude, the more so since I had at my disposal acting material which, albeit very responsive and versatile, was for the greatest part technically still completely unpolished. Indeed, I myself often stopped work, crossed out everything that had been done and started over from the beginning, because I felt that I was unwillingly falling now into the quagmire of the naturalistic theatre, now into the wax museum of the stylized.

Now I see clearly that it could not have been otherwise, that in the end no individual or even collective art, such as the theatre is, can free itself straight off from tradition. But at the time, naturally, it was nerve-wracking. I wanted to break with the past somewhat more quickly in order to forge new modes of creativity, to crystalize new grains of theatre in the crucible of our tireless search. Therefore, every success, every lucky breakthrough into the new theatre of our hopes increased our strength tenfold, and our cramped rehearsal room could have told of many nights when a fortuitously uttered intonation or a gesture discovered by chance chased away our fatigue and depression, and we greeted the dawn in cheerful work.

As a result of our rehearsals we succeeded in achieving an absolutely exceptional, almost religious aura of mystery. Now and then, especially in the scene of Shakuntala's farewell, we successfully transferred this to the stage, having transformed it into a rhythmic-theatrical plan and in this way gone beyond naturalistic "experiencing."

We also achieved significant successes in the area of form. The naked, painted bodies of the actors, moving in free rhythm, were a far cry from the artificially set bas-reliefs of the stylized theatre. The naked body unquestionably emancipated the actor and gave him more opportunity to achieve genuine emotionally-saturated form. But at the same time it also presented new difficulties. It became apparent immediately that if the majority of actors can just barely manage to wear contemporary costume appropriately and wear theatrical costume atrociously, they cannot manage their own bodies at all. A tremendous amount of work was necessary to get the actor to accept his body and learn to carry it with that uninhibited chastity in the presence of which the eye of the spectator did not dwell on the nudity but accepted it as an original and pleasing theatrical costume, as was the case during performances of *Shakuntala*.

Theatrical costume! This area, so brilliantly exploited by the artists of the stylized theatre, still seemed to be the sorest point with the new theatre. Beautiful, full of color, splendid and dynamic in the sketches, the costumes of even the best contemporary artists lose their lustre and hang formlessly when donned by an actor who allows them to oppress him and to impede his movement.

The principle of the revealed body helped us to solve the costume problems of *Shakuntala* with exceptional success. We constructed the costumes so that they did not hinder or distort gesture. On the contrary, they constantly underlined and vivified it, in movement and at rest, harmoniously merging with the actor's body and setting it off to scenic advantage. In my judgment the costumes for *Shakuntala* may well be among the most successfully executed of the last decade.

Unfortunately I cannot say the same for the setting. Perhaps in general it was interesting. Unquestionably there was some advancement here. Pavel Kuznetsov, whom I had attracted to the theatre for the first time, fulfilled the task presented him with great talent and a handsome and lavish use of color. [17] Nevertheless, it was not right, because I could not yet formulate those new principles of scenic construction which I felt intuitively, but for which I still had not found a concrete solution.

Certainly there was no place on the stage of the Kamerny Theatre for historical, naturalistic settings which reproduced Indian nature, castles, and temples. Nor was the Kamerny the place for the notorious "cloths" of the stylized theatre or its painted panels, against which the figure of the actor would be lost. We had to create a *scenic atmosphere* in which the lord of the stage, the actor, could create his art freely—an atmosphere which would not swallow up but rather would vivify the rhythmic alternation of forms as they unfolded logically and naturally on the stage, in the actual transfiguration of which lay the mystery of the play.

But how could it be created?

Should we take up the call of Meyerhold and Briusov and return to the theatre of antiquity? No. Until my theatrical plans had taken shape, I preferred to use the scheme of the Indian theatre. It was nearer to the play, less cumbersome, and to me more interesting. Rejecting the first sketches of P. Kuznetsov, who had executed them from a painter's point of view, I read to him, as my parting words, the following lines from Sylvain Levi: "The backdrop should be a curtain of fine material. Its color should harmonize with the basic feeling of the play: white for an erotic play, yellow for heroic, dark for pathetic, motley for comedy, black for tragedy, for horror—dark, for passion—red, and black for the marvelous."[18]

Taking these lines as a point of departure, we worked out the entire decorative plan of the production, granting ourselves of course complete creative freedom and certainly not setting ourselves to tasks of reconstruction. I was not tossing about between the Scylla of the naturalistic theatre (to which I also attribute the call to revival of the theatre of antiquity) and the Charybdis of the stylized theatre, only to fall into the moribund path of the theatre of reconstruction.

Our work was in full swing, now, and the time passed quickly. Besides our artistic worries we suffered through a million others, and finally, on the twelfth of December, 1914 (the memorable year of the beginning of the war) we opened the Kamerny Theatre.

Unfortunately, much that we had achieved in our rehearsal room was not transferred successfully to the stage. Because of construction we were unable to get onto the stage until a week before opening, and it was impossible to de-

"Shakuntala"

Alice Koonen as Shakuntala

lay the opening due to our lack of funds. *Shakuntala* appeared before the court of critics and public in an unfinished house, still wet with paint, and still reflecting and breaking up sound incorrectly. Much that had been discovered earlier was lost on the stage, and that which had been recovered had no time to jell.

But it had to be so.

Our instinct to preserve the theatre dictated this compromise. And we obeyed the command because we knew that we did so in the name of our future work, because we knew that the opening of the Kamerny was for us only a *beginning* of our unceasing search for the theatre of our hopes.

I will not dwell in detail on all the subsequent productions of the Kamerny Theatre. I will often have occasion to refer to them later on. Now I shall say only that two years of intensive work passed while we struggled to throw off the heavy burden of tradition. Finally we succeeded and presented *Famira Kifared,* in which appeared for the first time in a theatrically practical form the new systems of scenic construction and some of the new methods of acting which I had discovered. [19]

Naturally, over a period of two years there were precious flashes here and there of new designs, harmonies, rhythms, now in one, now in another production. But they were often so obscured by the husk of traditional form that they easily escaped the notice of the audience and elicited a response only from those earnest "parishioners" of our theatre who had trusted us from the beginning and demanded no proof.

Our frequent creative doubts were aggravated the whole time by the pressing circumstances in which we had to work. Our whole life was in essence a continuous fight for the survival of the theatre. Often I had to interrupt a rehearsal to replace a departed furnace man or to conduct torturous negotiations with creditors and shareholders of the theatre.* And if there was something extraordinary in the birth of the Kamerny Theatre, how much less accountable by any normal explanation is the fact that it could live and carry on its work with inhuman intensity in that murderous atmosphere of constant uncertainty which surrounded it for more than three years.

Under such conditions, under the catastrophic necessity to present without fail this or that play, to open on schedule no matter what, it is understandable that I often had to show unfinished works, striving to mount them as well as possible, to hide a little longer from uninitiated eyes all our secret discoveries,

---

*The exchange of a patron for a group of shareholders did not at all make it possible for us to work undisturbed as we had thought it would.

which were barely outlined and still in the process of work, so as to avoid the hasty boulevard appraisal which always fatally prostitutes everything it touches.

I remember with what arrogant cheap aestheticism the "clown tricks" of *The Fan* were exposed to public scorn by the same "arbiters" who loudly applaud the very same "tricks" in *Brambilla.* [20]

On the other hand, the eye-catching settings and costumes of Natalia Goncharova were accepted, if not with the enthusiasm which she undoubtedly deserved, in any case with patronizing praise, for like it or not one had to take into account that this was the same Natalia Goncharova who had created such a sensation in Paris with her *Golden Cockerel.* [21]

Even so the settings were too "radical" for the public, while for me they were simply the best possible compromise, the better taste of which was naturally mitigated by the fascinating talent of Goncharova. To me, in spite of all their "radicalness," they still reflected in many respects the period of the stylized theatre. I could not risk making a complete break with "settings" in the usual sense of the word and experiment with a new form of construction, because I was afraid that such a move would rock our boat even more, and as it was we were floundering hourly over every possible reef.

This temerity of mine was also reflected in the production of *The Marriage of Figaro,* [22] where a new kind of playing area had been worked out in rudimentary fashion, but the stage itself was decorated stylistically with the conventional screens, boskets, and curtains of S. Sudeikin. Such stage decoration obliged me to arrange a corresponding form of *mise-en-scène* and acting style. As a result, the whole play carried the stamp of "stylization," under the aesthetic varnish of which it was difficult to distinguish the outlines of new scenic rhythms and forms which had been incorporated into the production in various places.

But if for a long list of internal and external reasons I was temporarily forced to be satisfied with half measures in the area of scenic atmosphere, in the area of acting my situation was even more difficult. I had almost no actors capable of perceiving and fulfilling those new creative and technical tasks which arose more and more often in the process of our work.

In this regard the situation was truly tragic.

Those young people who set out with joyful willingness to meet my requirements proved to be completely unprepared raw material, necessitating colossal amounts of work in order even to approximate a fulfillment of my ideas. Actors with years of experience and so-called "technique" were so foreign to the very spirit of our work and so handicapped by their "experience" that in spite of a sincere desire to take part in work which was unusual for them, and even having achieved something or other in rehearsals, they invariably "rode their own pet horses" during performances and smashed to smithereens everything they had achieved. And were it not for the participation of Alice Koonen, that genuine enthusiast of the Kamerny Theatre, in the work and performances, were it not for her crystalization of a new craft of acting in the fiery conquest of obsolete methods, then not one of the ideas of theatre incorporated in my production plan would have crossed the footlights.

After many trials in this area I became firmly convinced that the Kamerny Theatre would be able to prove itself and become firmly established only when it trained and produced its own actors. It was impossible to find such actors on the outside, because work in all the existing theatres was carried on according to completely different systems. This meant that we would have to *create* our own actors.

The creation of such an actor could be effected only by way of special preparation and training under those special conditions laid down by our work. The creation of *our own school* became a matter of life and death for the Kamerny Theatre. So the school was created.

Work began to seethe with new vigor. All the misfortunes which befell us in such abundance were invariably broken on the firm will of our collective. The hypnotic effect of our steadily strengthening faith was so powerful that it subjugated even the incidental members of the theatre, and I shall never forget how in 1915 the whole troupe, composed entirely of impecunious people, gave up their wages to save the theatre. During the season of 1916-1917 all of us, with that ageless knight of the stage, the splendid Marius Mariusovich Petipa at the head,[23] cut our salaries to fifty rubles per month in order that the Kamerny might continue.

Nevertheless the fatal moment arrived.

On the twelfth of February, 1917, the farewell performance took place and the Kamerny Theatre died.

Did not solemn obituaries testify to the fact in all the papers? Did not a detailed article, "De Mortuis," confirm it in *Russkie Vedomosti,* which had always eschewed unconfirmed rumors? Did not Anatoli Kamensky's *Leda* blasphemously defile the holy stage of *Famira Kifared* a week later?

Nevertheless, the next fall playbills for the Kamerny Theatre hung once more from the telephone poles, giving notice of the opening of its season in a new location on Bolshaya Nikitskaya street, number 19, second court.

The 1917-1918 season was the turning point in our work.

We staged Oscar Wilde's *Salome,* a harlequinade, *King Harlequin* [by P. Lotara], the pantomime *Toy Box* by Debussy, and Paul Claudel's contemporary tragedy *l'Echange.* In these productions we broke decisively with both the naturalistic and the stylized theatre and set out at last on our own path, *the theatre of emotionally-saturated form,* the theatre which I define as *the theatre of neo-realism.*

Strange as it may seem, we were helped in our work during this year by the smallness of the quarters in which we had taken temporary refuge. Here we did not have to think about a whole raft of material cares connected with the conduct of a large theatre, which, in spite of our intentions, the theatre on Tverski Boulevard had turned out to be, and we were able to devote ourselves completely to our own work.

Now, after all the work of the theatre over a period of six years, after the significant and in many ways very fruitful work of our school, after having ourselves trained and established the nucleus of our own troupe, after the last productions of the past season, I consider myself justified in saying that the first period of the Kamerny Theatre, *the period of seeking its own way is ended.*

The second period now begins, a period no less difficult but no less alluring—*the period of uncovering the tremendous new possibilities languishing on this path,* the period of consolidation, the period of defining those new methods of creative acting and scenic construction the bases of which we have already indicated.

In order to make easier for me and my colleagues the work which lies before us, I shall try in the following pages to establish and, as it were, anchor those principles which have already been formulated in our work and outline those concepts and designs which are still maturing in our creative fantasy.

11. Dilettantism and Professional Excellence

If someone were to ask me which art is the most difficult, I should answer: the art of the actor. And if someone were to ask me which art is considered to be the easiest, I should answer again the art of the actor. Therein lies the clue to why acting continues to be the most underdeveloped, imperfect, and controversial of the arts: so controversial that there is even doubt whether in fact it is an art; so imperfect that Eleonora Duse dreams of the destruction of all actors by the plague; so underdeveloped that Gordon Craig insists repeatedly that "the theatre will continue to grow, and actors for many years to come will continue to hinder its development."*

This condition will undoubtedly continue until we categorically put an end to that frivolous and criminal attitude toward the art of the actor which for various reasons has taken root in the contemporary theatre. Who in fact does not dare to mount the stage these days? And who, having barely stepped onto the field, does not dare "to tackle Shakespeare"?

In order to play the piano even tolerably well, it is considered necessary that one work day after day for tens of years, and this not in order to become a concert pianist but only to play in one's spare time for one's own enjoyment or for one's husband, or at the most for two or three "family" auditors. But in order to act on the stage, publicly, before the eyes of a thousand spectators, it is considered completely sufficient "to have the call." And what does it matter if you do not articulate half the sounds, if your voice grates like bars in a rusty lock, if your gestures are confused like the legs of a tired horse, if you have not the slightest notion of the methods and objectives of the craft of acting. In

*Gordon Craig, "The Actor and the Super-marionette."

such cases it is pointed out simply that you are "getting broken in," just as one would speak of a horse, and the cynical process of accumulating acting experience in public begins, along with the presumptuous simulation of a mastery which is lacking.

Is it any wonder after this that Duse in despair called down a plague upon all actors and that Craig pined wistfully for a super-marionette?

Naturally, it is very easy to say, as did Craig, "the actor must go, and his place will be taken by an inanimate figure—let's call it a super-marionette." But then where is the theatre? After all, the marionette, even the super-marionette, was not invented by Craig. It has its own history, as old as the world, as mysterious as a fetish, as beautiful as death. And nevertheless the theatre always created alongside the marionette its own special art. For the essence of theatre has always been *action*, the unique vehicle for which has unfailingly been an *actively functioning* person, i.e., an actor.

Passive motion has always been the lot of the marionette, in spite of all the mysterious power inherent in it, and only the active will of a neurotic can convert this movement into a phantasmagoric semblance of action. In this difference lies an unbridgeable gulf; and like two quite similar but parallel lines which will never merge, the art of the marionette and the art of the theatre, in spite of their often striking resemblance, can never trade places. And that is why Craig's supplication for "a return to the theatre of the idol, the super-marionette" must remain forever unanswered.

I am not saying simply that the super-marionette cannot *return* to the theatre because in fact it never was in the theatre. I am saying that in any case it is not capable of replacing the actor. This being the case, is it not better to "pray" for a return to the theatre of its real idol, the actor—or, if you will, the *super-actor*, to differentiate him from the wretched creatures who now call themselves actors? This kind of praying comes a good deal harder, but it will breathe life back into the theatre.

The contemporary theatre is shot through with *dilettantism*, like a moth-eaten cloak which is passed down from generation to generation. And if we do not immediately make a superhuman effort, its riddled fabric will soon be good for nothing but a shroud.

Dilettantism! Cursed enemy of the contemporary, especially the Russian, theatre—cunning and crafty, a werewolf, assuming various but always respectable identities. If you scrape down to the kernel of that celebrated acting "interior" for which Kugel tearfully pined and in the name of which even Belinsky composed hymns,[1] you will see hiding under the last layer of husk the smug grimace of dilettantism. If you were to dissect the clumsy verisimilitude of the naturalistic theatre or the stiff, sterile artifice of the stylized theatre or the slick "proficiency" of the market theatre, in every case you would find lurking the old, familiar face of dilettantism.

And yet I doubt whether it is possible to name another art which by its very nature has less in common with dilettantism than acting, since of all the arts it is 'undoubtedly the most complicated and difficult. Indeed, in every other art, particularly the plastic arts, the creator and his creative personality, the material, the instrument, and the work of art which is the end of the whole creative process are separate one from the other, so that the material, the instrument, and the work itself stand *outside* the creative personality. *Only in acting are the creative personality, the material, the instrument, and the work of art itself combined in a single entity, being organically incapable of separation.*

This fundamental condition, which constitutes a sharp distinction between the art of the actor and every other art, and which establishes for acting absolutely unique difficulties, is, it seems to me, perfectly clear in and of itself. But when verified by examples, it becomes especially striking. You, painter, your creative ego is an artist, a creative personality which in the last analysis creates the work of art. But the material with which you create—colors, canvas, etc.; your instruments—brushes, easel, etc.; and the created work itself—a painting, fresco, scenery, all these are outside you. They lie before you; you are free to select them, test them, combine and alter them as you please, for they are not part of you, and you are free, as it were, to appraise them from the side.

The same phenomenon characterizes every other art with the single exception of acting.

You, actor, your ego is a creative personality who conceives and translates into reality a work of your art; but you yourself, your body—your hands, feet, torso, head, eyes, voice, speech—are that material out of which you create your work; you yourself—your muscles, joints, ligaments—are also the necessary instrument; and your entire being, embodied in a scenic image, is, finally, that work of art which is born of the whole creative process.

You are everything; everything is embodied in you; everything is achieved through you.

And if long years of study and unremitting practice are needed to master any given art, then what a quantity of will, work, and training must be applied to master the most difficult, complicated, and capricious of all arts—the art of the actor. For if in every other art you are always free to choose the material most suitable to your intent (clay, marble, granite, bronze, silver, etc.), here you are stuck with the material fate has given you, and from it only may you sculpt those images crying to you for birth. And this material which is at your disposal is without doubt the most capricious, subject to every kind of accident, changeable, unstable, short-lived. What tireless vigilance, what consummate craft must you master, actor, in order to subjugate this "material" to your creative will and force it obediently to assume—and often maintain for years—a given form.

The extreme dependence of the actor's art on the nature of his material was acknowledged long ago—indeed, with the very birth of the theatre. Witness, for instance, the demands made of the actor in ancient India: " . . . freshness, beauty, a pleasant, broad face, red lips, beautiful teeth, a neck round as a bracelet, beautifully formed hands, graceful build, powerful hips, charm, grace, dignity, nobility, pride, not to speak of the quality of talent."[*]

It is sufficient to compare these stringent requirements of the Indian theatre with the picture presented by the contemporary theatre in this regard in order to be convinced how deeply the corrupting poison of dilettantism has penetrated our art and how more and more it is deforming our material. The chief share of the blame for this situation undoubtedly falls to the naturalistic theatre, which in its anti-artistic striving to make the theatre like life, threw open the stage doors to such material as might truly reflect the degeneration of the human body in contemporary life.

Meanwhile, not so long ago, still within our memory, there were and often still are actors who understand the tremendous significance of their material to the art of acting and know how to care for it. I shall never forget how enraged Marius Petipa once became during a dress rehearsal for *Figaro* when the younger members of the company, struck by the strong, youthful appearance of his legs, suspected that his tights were padded. Not waiting for the end of the rehearsal, he called everyone to his dressing room, took off his tights and confidently displayed his legs, which truly would be the envy of any of our present youth. When in amazement they all began to question how he had been able to preserve his body so well for over sixty years, he, half joking, answered that he possessed the secret of eternal youth. Alas, there was a measure of truth in his answer; for the contemporary actor-dilettante it unfortunately is a secret. But of course it is no secret from the ballet artists, the only ones among contemporary actors who value and take care of their material.

[*]Sylvain Levi, *Le Théâtre Indien.*

The fact that the work of art he is creating cannot be separated from himself also presents considerable difficulties to the actor. While every other artist, both in the process of work and after its completion, being separate from the work he is creating, can at any moment physically see it, check it, varying as he chooses the point of view, distance, light—the actor lacks this important resource. In order to compensate for this lack and not be condemned to blindness, he must develop in himself an inner second sight; he must create alongside his own creative ego a second ego, unseen but seeing.

And so the art of acting, besides all the difficulties which lie in the path of any art, presents to the actor still other, unique tasks, requiring special means of mastery.

Hence it is clear that to want to act, to have a "calling" for it, even talent, is far from being enough to actually become an actor. No, a tremendous amount of preparatory work and continuous training is necessary to turn your vague wish into professional excellence, so that in the end you are not a *wunderkind* or a talented dilettante but a true *actor, a master of your art.*

It requires work, work, and more work.

It requires a school.

I have already said that the only actors in the contemporary theatre who understand the importance of their material to their art are the actors of the ballet. Certainly they are the only ones who have their own school, and generally speaking they are the only ones until recently to be master-actors. I do not mean to imply by this, however, that I accept the contemporary ballet in its entirety. Not at all. It is true that I love it and value it highly. Ballet productions are the only examples of the contemporary theatre in which I can still experience genuine creative joy and excitement. But that does not prevent me from recognizing at the same time its tremendous shortcomings; nor does it prevent me from sensing how the corrosive rust of routine and the formalism which lurks behind the beautiful mask of classicism threaten to corrupt even this art, until now left relatively intact.

Nevertheless, neither the one-sided character of the technique cultivated in the ballet, nor its archaic methods of mimicry, nor its mechanical "motor" approach to the creative process itself, nor its many other defects can overshadow in my eyes the still-preserved fundamental fact and predominant advantage of the ballet stage—the mastery of its actors. They are not dilettantes; they have a *right to the stage,* a right earned through school, work, and a tireless striving for perfection. Every one of them has gone through school, working on the preparation of his instrument for six to seven years, and continues to work unceasingly up to his last hour on the stage. They are not at all all geniuses, all talented, all equally gifted; nor, of course, do all of them become ballerinas, soloists, or chorus leaders. The less gifted or the not yet sufficiently virtuosic form the corps de ballet, that amazing group of masters. Thanks to them the ballet stage is the only one in the contemporary theatre to be protected from dilettantism and to remain in the sphere of genuine art—where everyone on the stage is not a "casual colleague" but a trained master, on a level with the others who have passed through the complex school of their beautiful art.

So must it be in theatre art as a whole and in every branch of it; and just as in the ballet there is a corps de ballet, so in the dramatic theatre, along with the heroes and heroines, must there be a corps de drama, whose members, just as in the ballet, are confident masters of their art. Only under such conditions may the theatre be revitalized; only under such conditions will genuine art ascend the throne of the stage and not its surrogate in the form of dilettantism, however talented, elevated into a "system."

Two basic processes, interweaving in millions of inscrutable ways, invariably accompany the creation of any work of art: the process of the internal formation of the artist's intent and the process of its external embodiment. If for the external embodiment of his vision the artist must master his instrument and material, for its internal formation he must master his creative will and his ability to call up in himself and to make articulate the emotions which give birth to that vision.

These processes are of course characteristic also of the creative activity of the actor. However, for the actor, both in the area of internal formation of intent and the area of its external embodiment, there lie in wait still other difficulties which are peculiar to his art alone. For the fact is that if the necessary emotion temporarily diminishes or the creative will becomes inert, every other artist may lay his brush or chisel aside for a while and await a more suitable time to continue his work. Only the actor lacks this possibility. Even in rehearsals, when quite properly the creation of the scenic image is still incomplete, the actor, owing to the collective character of his art, lacks that freedom which is available to every other artist. In order not to hold up the general creative process, he must be able at any given moment to arouse his creative will and call up the necessary emotions. But in still greater degree is this ability necessary to him in production, when at the predetermined moment of the opening sary to him in production, when at the predetermined moment of the opening of the curtain the irrevocable course of the performance begins. True, the actor brings to the performance an already prepared scenic image, but there is a burdensome peculiarity in his insatiable art: in order that this already created form ring true, in order that there be on the stage not a dead *moulage* but an emotionally saturated form, the actor, with an unheard-of lavishness of creativity, must give it flesh and blood anew with every performance.

Accordingly, the actor must be in perfect control not only of his instrument and material but also of his creative will and his ability effortlessly to call up in himself at any given moment the requisite gamut of emotions. Hence a categorical necessity: the actor must command equally not only the external technique which permits him to give to a preconceived scenic image the desired form, but also the internal technique which gives him the capacity to saturate this form with the emotions which engendered it.

Two techniques, internal and external, lie in the path of the actor who will master his art, the path which will lead to a new, a master actor.

III. The Actor's Internal Technique

It is common knowledge that the actor's internal technique, the tremendous significance of which is of course indisputable, was assiduously cultivated by the naturalistic theatre, which considered so-called *"perezhivanie"* and the knack of its control to be of paramount importance.[1] And indeed, being absolutely helpless in the area of external technique, the naturalistic theatre seems to have achieved a high degree of perfection in the area of internal technique, wherein, by general admission, lies the bulk of its power over an audience.

But this is true only in so far as one speaks of "perezhivanie" in general, as one of the psychic resources of any human being. One need only remember that in the present context the discussion concerns not "pereshivanie" in the general sense of the word, but "perezhivanie" in a special sense—as that creative emotion which is one of the elements of the art of the actor—and all the illusory perfection of the naturalistic theatre at once falls apart, since it is built on an essentially faulty foundation.

According to the demand of the naturalistic theatre, "perezhivanie" must be based on the affective memory of a corresponding emotional experience from the personal life of the performer or an observation of the required emotional experience in others. In either case it must without fail meet the requirement of *truth to life*. The *lifelikeness* of "perezhivanie" is the alpha and omega of the naturalistic gospel. But this very vital power of the process is at the same time its fundamental defect, for it robs "perezhivanie" of whatever creative basis it may have had and transfers it from the region of art to the region of psychopathology.

There is absolutely no need to be an actor in order to experience emotion-

ally in a lifelike fashion, for lifelike "perezhivanie" is not at all a specific peculiarity of the stage. Imagine a bullfight, for instance, at that moment when the
wounded toreador is dying in the arena. Certainly no one doubts that his emotional experiencing of death is sincere and lifelike. On the contrary, it possesses to the maximum degree all the characteristics which make it most valuable
from the point of view of the naturalistic theatre. But does that make this an
artistic phenomenon; is "emotional experiencing" here an element in the creativity of an actor? No. For that, "experiencing" obviously must possess other
characteristics besides sincerity and vitality. Otherwise, as Coquelin rightly
says, "If actors must cry in order to make others cry, then logic demands that
they get tight when playing drunks, and that in order to represent a murderer
they ask some hypnotist to implant in them the impulse to stab a comrade—or
at least the prompter."*

An incident which Coquelin describes from his personal life is extremely
interesting and significant in this regard:

> It was during a tour. I had spent the whole night on the train, rehearsed in the
> morning, and then went for an outing on foot.
>   That evening I played Hannibal in *Avanturiere.* As you know, at the end of the
> second act Hannibal, whom Fabrice is trying to get drunk so that he will talk, first
> gets drunk and then falls asleep. I played the drunken scene as usual, no better no
> worse. But no sooner had I gotten into the sleep scene but that what I was imitat-
> ing seemed so pleasant, I so wanted to sleep, that without realizing it I succumbed
> to the temptation, fell asleep on the stage before the public, and even—shameful—
> began to snore.**

Coquelin's emotional experiencing of sleep was without doubt sufficiently sincere and lifelike. But it is just as certain that from the moment this completely
lifelike emotional experience began, he ceased to be an actor, having lost all
contact with art.

This is the inevitable and fatal destiny of "perezhivanie" which is based on
truth to life. It leads the actor away from art and makes of him a morbid person, a neurasthenic, with the obstinacy of a maniac, wallowing about in his
own soul and carrying out home experiments in psychology.

Furthermore, as I have already said, in order to master such "perezhivanie"
it is not at all necessary to be an actor, that is to say a person distinguished by
some special gift or talent. With a modicum of observational power and a cer-

*Coquelin the Elder, *The Art of the Actor.*
**Ibid.*

tain nervous excitability or a light disorder of the nervous system, anyone can learn to "experience emotionally" in such a fashion. Nor is it necessary to complete any kind of creative act; it is necessary only to overcome one's healthy human shyness and to force oneself to do right in front of people that which of course it is much more natural to do apart from them, in private.

In the last analysis, is this not what even the Second Studio of the Moscow Art Theatre based its work on, particularly the notorious *Green Ring*? [2] This spring, when I talked with its members about the goals and path of the new theatre and about the education of the new actor, I said that I could undertake with no less success than they to stage *The Green Ring* with any high-school graduating class. And I still say it. For when a high-school student is asked to be on the stage—just as in life—a high-school student, he needs to do only one thing: overcome his natural shyness. Everything else can easily be achieved in a hundred or two rehearsals (I do not know how many there were in the studio).

Indeed, to be quite frank, *The Green Ring* was performed in the Second Studio by just such high-school students—or in any case girls and boys still young enough to remember the joys of noon recess. They had just barely mounted the stage; when had they time to master the most complicated of the arts? How could they suddenly, without any preparation, become actors?

Of course, they were not actors. That is not necessary in order to learn how to "experience emotionally" in lifelike fashion and turn up on the stage of a naturalistic theatre. For in essence it is not a theatre, and the work performed there is not true theatre art. It was not for nothing that during its tour in St. Petersburg the Art Theatre arranged performances in which the actors did not act but only "experienced emotionally," reading the plays as they sat around a table. But if this is so, then why, notwithstanding, does the naturalistic theatre command an audience, and by what means does it still, at least to some extent, hold that audience in lingering captivity?

I will not concern myself here with the ideological side of this question. I will not attempt to explain how the audience found in this theatre, or rather in the literature which this theatre had taken over, answers to those "cursed questions" which tormented them, and how it was this which in large measure attracted the audience within its walls. I am here interested in something else.

It must certainly be admitted that the naturalistic theatre captures not only the mind but the whole being of the spectator and that the "experiencing" of the naturalistic theatre, which can in no way be admitted to have artistic value, nevertheless attracts the spectator into its circle with considerable power. It must also be admitted that it is precisely this which explains the audience's great devotion to the naturalistic theatre, since otherwise, having an instinctive feeling for art, the audience would long ago have forsaken it and its truth. For of course Coquelin was right when he said that if there were any place where truth may not be verisimilar it is on the stage.

Wherein lies the power of the naturalistic theatre? It lies in the fact that its "experiencing" is psychological and triggers a corresponding *physiological infection* in the spectator, appealing to his lowest but, if you will, most powerful instincts.* An analogous excitement grips the audience during a bullfight upon the death of the toreador, during a knightly joust, or when one is witnessing an execution. It is not for nothing that the Spanish Inquisition made a public show of its executions and that a bullfight is always staged like a theatrical performance.

When a live human being is dying in front of you, writhing in torment, is it not all the same to you whether he is a gladiator or an actor "living the part?" You experience the same physiological excitement, the more so when the theatre obligingly meets you halfway by not opening the curtain at the end of the performance so as not to disturb the "illusion" which has arisen in you and which it blasphemously calls an "artistic effect." With respect to such a theatre, Gordon Craig was of course right when he asserted that a furious melee between an elephant and a tiger gives us the same excitement we may receive from the contemporary stage and gives it to us in its pure form. But he was absolutely wrong when he supposed this to be a flaw of the theatre in general, and that the only way out was to replace the actor by a marionette. No, it is not the marionette but the living actor, the actor-creator, the actor-master who must and undoubtedly can evoke in the audience not physiological but other feelings—feelings which lie in the sphere of genuine art and its true perception. But in order to do so he must once and for all renounce that physiological "perezhivanie" of the naturalistic theatre, which is on a completely different plane.

For the actor, "true" emotion does not at all need to be lifelike, nor must it feed on things dredged up out of other people. Nor, of course, on the other hand, need it be stylized, for the schematized portrayal of emotion is just as inimical to the creativity of the actor as is physiological "experiencing."

*I am using the term "physiological *perezhivanie*" figuratively, in the sense that all artistic terminology is figurative.

"Every art has its element of realism and its stylization," writes V. Briusov in his article "Realism and Stylization on the Stage." "The visible side of an art work, on which the primary attention of any given art is concentrated, must be executed with all the realism at its disposal. So must the play of an actor be realistic, but this realism must not cross over into naturalism."[3]

Yes, the play of an actor must undoubtedly be realistic. It cannot be otherwise, for all the material of his art is real, the form of its embodiment is real, its emotion is real. But real scenic emotion must draw its sustenance not from real life (the actor's or someone else's) but from the *created* life of that *scenic figure* which the actor has called up to creative being from the magical land of fantasy. Wilde says somewhere that the man who does not have hanging on his wall a geographical map with a country by the name of "fantasy' on it is not worthy of the name "man." In any case, he is not worthy of the name "artist," "actor." It is in that legendary land of fantasy that the actor must bring to life those scenic figures which are the products of his art.

The scenic figure is a synthesis of emotion and form brought to life by the creative fantasy of the actor.

A scenic figure of emotionally saturated form may be created only by a new, synthetic theatre; the naturalistic theatre has produced only physiological emotion without form; the stylized theatre—only external form, devoid of emotion.

The first stage of that process, the stage of seeking a scenic image, yields to no definite rules or system. This stage, deeply individual, is different for each actor, and the secret of the birth of the scenic figure is just as wonderful, just as inscrutable as the secret of life and death. Were it possible to discover this secret, to analytically dissect it and put it back together, then art would cease to exist; the artistic act would become an analytic one.

Of course the director may and must help the actor in the process of seeking a form for his character, but he must do so with extreme care, tactfully adapting himself to the individuality of the actor, since different actors feel their way through this process in different ways. Even the same actor in exploring different roles may often proceed by diametrically opposite paths, and if in one case he may be led to the sought-for image, let us say, by a pantomimic approach, in another he may with great success use the sense of sound as his point of departure, and in a third some internal emotion which suddenly catches fire, etc., etc.

Only when the actor already feels the image within himself may the so-called "work on the role" begin, which is the second basic stage in the actor's creativity. This stage is considerably easier since it lends itself to precise calculation and is subject to a definite plan, which is part of the pattern of action assigned to a character in a given play. Here, in the action of the play, in the encounter with other characters, the scenic image which the actor feels within him is forged into a corresponding visible and distinct form, thus completing the creative process of the actor. From this moment on, the scenic image may be considered complete, and the actor, being in complete command of it, can play without difficulty *any role offered him in that image.* In other words, the actor in this way once again becomes master of that self-contained power of theatrical art which was cultivated so intensively in the characters of the commedia dell'arte.

In such a sequence of work it will be easy for the actor to find the emotions necessary for action without running the risk that they will be emotions from life (ones which feed off of his own past experiences or the experiences of those close to him). They will be genuine, *original emotions, creatively transformed through the given scenic figure.* Such emotions will not smell of physiological sweat, and the "infection" they initiate in the spectator will of course be different from that triggered by the notorious "perezhivanie."* It will be an artistic effect, an effect arising within the aesthetic plan, an effect capable of moving the audience to both joy and tears, but in the same way in which they are moved by the sculpture of Praxiteles or the *Requiem* of Mozart.

In his article on the theatre, enumerating the methods of scenic performance he has unearthed, Meyerhold demands of the actor "tragedy with a smile." It seems to me that a smile must indeed play a part in moments of tragic tension in the theatre, but not on the face of the actor, rather on the face or in the soul of the spectator. By this I mean to say that during moments of the most tragic cataclysms on the stage, a smile must flicker in the soul of even the most shaken spectator—a smile born of delight with the work of art being created before his eyes, a feeling which he must inevitably experience even in the most tragic moments.

So far it has been primarily in the ballet that one could experience such a feeling. Recall *Giselle* for instance. If you saw Pavlova, you will never forget the beautiful moment of her death, stunning in the authenticity of its tragedy. And still, shaken though you were, a smile invariably blossomed in your soul—

*Naturally the element of physiology will still be present, but it will not play such a domineering and self-important role as in the "perezhivanie" of the naturalistic theatre.

a smile of delight at the joy Pavlova's incomparable art had given you—a smile because it was not she who was dying but the scenic image created by her art which was flickering out before your eyes.

Last season *Adrienne Lecouvreur* was staged in the Kamerny theatre.* Perhaps you remember the finale of the piece. Adrienne dies from poisoned flowers at the very moment when her beloved Maurice has returned to invite her to a life perfumed with all the flowers of good fortune. Under the sorrowful strains of the *Marche Funebre* a beautiful life expires, and the audience is stricken by the terrible pain of bereavement.

I waited impatiently for the end of the dress rehearsal; I wanted to verify whether besides the sense of death there would also arise in the auditorium a smile at the art being created. It did. I was pleased to feel it and to recognize it in a number of people, among them those in whose theatrical sensibility I had absolute faith.

I was pleased to find this out because I place no value on theoretical constructions not tempered in the efficacious fire of the theatre. And now with even greater conviction than before, I contend that Gordon Craig is making a fundamental error when he assures us that "the actor is completely at the mercy of emotion," that "in one instant, like lightning, before reason has time to cry out in protest, seething passion has already seized command of all the actor's means of expression. . . . He is wholly in the power of emotion and ready to cry to it, 'Do with me what you will.'" All this is to a large degree true when one is dealing with naturalistic "experiencing." Here, having stimulated his own nervous system, the actor often loses control of it and even falls himself under its influence. But one should view this as a *morbid phenomenon,* engendered not by emotion but by an incorrect approach to it. On the other hand, emotion which has been transformed by a scenic figure is by that very transformation freed from such morbidness and is easily controlled by the actor, who has called it up by his own creative will.

The development of the creative will and the creative fantasy, the ability to entice from it any scenic figure, to call up and control the necessary emotions—these comprise the internal technique of the actor. The route to it lies for the most part through *improvisation.*

Improvisation embraces an infinite number of exercises which discipline the creative will, develop the fantasy, and so forth. However, since improvisation is also practiced both in the naturalistic and stylized theatres, I should like

*Alice Koonen played Adrienne.

to mention two groups of exercises separately. I am speaking of exercises on "the object" and on "emotion."

The naturalistic theatre teaches the actor to have an object within the stage area (an internal object, a partner, some thing), deliberately excluding the auditorium as an object. The stylized theatre, on the other hand, ignoring the partner as object, directs the actor exclusively to the auditorium. Our new theatre must combine these objects. While associating with his partner, the actor must at the same time be aware that before him is an auditorium, not the fourth wall of naturalism.

Improvisation in the synthetic theatre must lead the actor to a mastery of this dual object. With respect to exercises on emotion, it is necessary to reach the point where emotion arises not of itself but arises dependent upon the stage task of a given character. Only under such a condition can it be transformed from naturalistic "experiencing" into a creative phenomenon lying within the designs of our art.

IV.   The Actor's External Technique

As I have said, the mastery of internal technique alone does not give the actor the potential to create a finished scenic figure. In order to complete the entire creative process and make the work of scenic art being created by him visible to the spectator, the actor must shape it into a corresponding form, making use of such material as he has at his disposal.

We already know that for the actor his own body—his breath, his voice, his entire physical being—serves as this material. The ability to make use of this material comprises the external technique of the actor.

Without a virtuosic command of this technique, without that free mastery which is indispensable in this area, all the actor's most brilliant intentions, all his most daring and inspired internal images are doomed to failure. Struggling against unmanageable and unresponsive material, they will not find their form and will not reach the audience, or will reach it as if reflected in a warped mirror, in a distorted and mutilated condition.

This, it seems to me, is already clear in itself. The following brief but striking example cited by Delsarte is intended for those who still have not grasped this absolute truth: An actor is making a declaration of love on the stage. A sincere and fiery emotion is burning in his heart. But he is not master of his material, and his body, left to its own devices, reflects its own sensations. His romantic agitation is manifest externally in the intense shaking of his legs, and as a result the auditorium roars with laughter. Not only did the actor's true emotion not reach the audience, but just the opposite: the inappropriate trembling of his legs, i.e., a *false form,* distorted the image itself, giving it characteristics which the actor would rather have avoided.

I, too, and probably many of you could cite cases when an actor or actress

has sincerely wept on the stage and evoked only laughter or at the best indif-
ference. One could cite many other examples, but I think it unnecessary. The
Pushkin production at the Art Theatre and the particularly tragic illustration
of this in *Cain* speak better and clearer than any words. [1]

So, the actor must master his material; he must come to know it, to love it,
and to develop it to the point where it becomes flexible, dependable, and obedient to his will. Like an enchanted Stradivarius, the body of the actor must
respond to the slightest pressure of his creative fingers, obediently embodying
in an efficient flow of clear-cut forms the most delicate vibrations of his creative desire.

To achieve this a tremendous amount of work and tireless daily training is
necessary. Actors should take inspiration from a brilliant master such as
Rubenstein. When he was on tour he took a dummy keyboard with him in the
railroad car so as not to let a day pass without practicing. In just such fashion
must the actor work to overcome his inherent lack of plastic expression, to
master his capricious and constantly changing material.

The body of the contemporary actor is not a Stradivarius but a three-string-
ed balalaika, on which he can just barely manage to play *Chizhika* or some
similar street song, but which proves to be completely unsuitable for the transmission of other more complicated harmonies. The actor needs long and serious
training in order to develop his body and learn how to master it.

Of course the best thing would be to open a school for children seven to
eight years old and develop new actors from them. The most gifted would become heroes and heroines, leading men and leading ladies. The rest would form
that indispensable *corps-de-théâtre* of my dreams, without which genuine scenic art is altogether unthinkable. Only with the formation of such a corps will
it be possible at last to remove from the face of the theatre that shameful blemish which erupts whenever in so-called mass scenes its boards are crowded by a
casual band of "supers" with whose help Messrs. Directors construct their
"brilliant productions."

But this path, being very long, risks being sterile as well, since a good
twenty to twenty-five years will pass before a theatre grows from such a school,
and in our art only that work succeeds which comes in contact hourly with the
active combustion of a theatrical operation, testing its achievements in the fire.
Therefore, I decided to experiment with a school into which, after a prelimi-
nary test, we would take young people primarily between sixteen and twenty
years of age, introducing into their studies those disciplines by means of which,

in my view, the maximum results might be achieved. Along with lessons in body movement and ballet-gymnastics, which develop the body in only one direction and in the last analysis do not give it that freedom of movement which is so necessary to the actor, I introduced lessons in fencing, acrobatics, and juggling.

I smile now as I remember with what mockery this was met in theatre circles, how they spoke about the actors of the Kamerny Theatre learning to be jumping jacks, how they said that actors had no business being "clowns," that all this was deliberate affectation. I remember how a reviewer in *Russkie Vedomosty* (apparently not realizing the praise contained in his words) wrote of Alice Koonen as Minerva, in *The Azure Carpet,*[2] that she did not act but danced her role, how in some "model" theatres the most scathing rebuke to an actor was, "You are putting on Kamerny airs," etc., etc.

Of course, this mocking did not disturb us, and while the venerable theatrical circles laughed complacently, we worked, constantly verifying our work

"Princess Brambilla"

"Princess Brambilla"

in active scenic creativity. After a short time the attitude toward the studies we had introduced changed sharply. Individual theatre big-wigs and whole theatrical collectives were forced to admit their undoubted value and even began introducing corresponding studies into their own training programs. The production of *Princess Brambilla* played the role of the most conclusive argument on this issue.

In my public conversations about this production, by the way, I said that in this respect *Princess Brambilla* was a spectacle for the blind, since in it even they must see at last what tremendous, absolutely untapped possibilities the mastery of his material opens up to the actor. And this at a time when we had only taken the first tentative steps in that direction. How mighty, many-faceted, and beautiful will the actor be when he has followed this route to the achievement of genuine perfection.

So, from my point of view, the experiment I conducted produced the desired results. It convinced me that the human body both in its youth and even later on can yield sufficiently to training and may be led to a comparatively higher degree of perfection.

Of course this does not abrogate my intention to organize a school for children also, but it finally confirms in fact my long-held conviction that Gordon Craig is absolutely wrong in asserting that "acting is not an art" because in order to create any work of art we must work only with material whose behavior can be predicted, and the human being does not belong to that class of material. This is of course not true, and the fallacy could have been demonstrated earlier by the example of the acrobat if nothing else. Does not his material, i.e., his body, yield itself to the most precise calculation? Can there be any place for "chance" when he performs his exercises and vaults at the very top of the circus dome, when the slightest accident, the most insignificant disobedience of the body, i.e., departure from the predicted pattern of response, threatens inevitable death? How can one say after this example that the human body is not suitable as material for the theatre?

"But," one may object, "that is the circus; there they do not play those emotional roles which according to Craig cause the actor to lose his equilibrium."

My answer is that this is not true, since the acrobat is without doubt an actor as well, and in any case is not a mechanical doll. Prove to me that the sense of contact with death which inevitably arises in him thanks to the constant possibility of falling is in any way weaker than those emotions by which the actor is sometimes possessed. In my opinion it is even more difficult to cope with than true scenic emotion, because by its very nature it approximates physiological "experiencing." Nevertheless, the acrobat does not let it overwhelm him and confuse the necessary patterns of behavior. He subjugates it to his will, and with the help of his material—his body—executes that "predetermined design" without which, according to Craig's just observation, art may not be born.

There is no doubt that the actor on the stage can quite easily subjugate to his creative will both his emotions and his material. I assert this now with the utmost conviction on the basis of experiments I have conducted in the theatre in various scenic exercises as well as in production, and particularly in *Princess Brambilla*. At the same time I repeat that those experiments were conducted with actors and students who were taking only the first steps along that difficult path toward mastery of internal and external acting technique.

Along with the mastery of his body, the actor must of course achieve no less degree of mastery over his voice and diction. And it may be that this area presents even greater difficulties than that which has been the subject of discussion up to now. For if, in the area of the body, we have in the past not been without some kind of anchors which we might lay hold of to lighten our work, here, in the area of voice and diction, our path is blocked by troublesome and firmly imbedded habits which must first be overcome before we can arrive at the desired results. Many frustrations still await us here, but of course that fact cannot diminish the fervor of our quest, the less so since here also we have already achieved some things which will undoubtedly help us in our further work.

Following the example of the naturalistic theatre, the contemporary stage is dominated by expressionless, timbreless, "every-day" voices and the horrible, vulgar, "lifelike" diction of the man in the street. It has become the obligatory sign of the actor with "good taste." To tell an actor that he speaks simply and naturally is to play him the nicest of compliments. As Coquelin writes,

> Don't talk to me about those who will not pronounce distinctly, who babble before the public as though they were at table, who hesitate, correct themselves, repeat words, cut them off like the ends of so many cigars, mumble and transform the words of the author into some kind of mush. I know that the actor may earn a reputation for great naturalness by imitating the tone of simple conversation, by not pronouncing one word louder than another, by swallowing the ends of phrases, stuttering, abbreviating, giving the impression that he cannot express himself. He repeats two and three times in a row, speaks in a monotone for ten minutes at a time, then suddenly increases his rate of speech in order to build more quickly to the punch line. And the undiscriminating public exclaims, "Good Lord, what naturalness! One would think he were at home. What an actor! I did not hear, did you? But how naturally it was uttered!"

One must give Coquelin credit; it would be difficult to ridicule more astutely that horrifying *stamp of simplicity* which has built itself such a firm nest on the contemporary stage. And of course Coquelin is right when he says that such actors are destined to play only in the current pieces. When this stamp of simplicity is applied to other kinds of plays, its antipathy to art is revealed with even greater strength.

But though I reject this studied simplicity, which by the way is undoubtedly the easiest mode of speech, I certainly do not call for that "cold coinage of words," where, according to the thesis of Meyerhold, "words must fall like drops into a deep well." No. Just as I seek the complete liberation and development of the actor's body in order that it may freely cast itself into any creatively conceived form, so I wish to liberate and develop the actor's voice and diction so that every scenic figure may impart to them its own special sound and pattern of speech. Just as the body gives the scenic figure its plastic form, so voice and diction must give it phonetic form.

There is no place in art for chance. Nor must there be anything fortuitous in the speech of the actor; it must be in the strictest *rhythmic* accord with the whole image being created. This is the first and chief requirement. Everything else, the logical as well as the psychological structure of speech, must give way before the rhythmic.

"The phonetic power of words," says Jean d'Udin, "is a mighty implement for influencing the imagination, and if anyone denies this and, disregarding the expressiveness of the sounds of words, contends that the etymological meaning is stronger than the phonetic, let him close this book; we never will agree in the area of art."*

"By pronouncing well and observing rhythm, one can give some kind of poetic nuance to even the most vulgar prose," writes Coquelin, "but here, on the contrary, they contrive to impart to poetry the characteristics of prose. It is difficult to recall without a feeling of indignation how in the contemporary theatre they deliver verse 'naturally,' mangling the form, meter and rhythm of the poet to satisfy the demands of 'lifelikeness.' "

Coquelin's derision of such a manner of delivering verse is particularly apt: "They delivered the verse of *Athalie* as we say 'Hello, how are you.' 'Yes, yes, my Lord,' mumbles Abner, 'I have come to the temple to pay respects to the most High One [casually, as though with walking stick in hand], to celebrate with you [in friendly fashion] that great day when on Mount Sinai [if I am not mistaken] we were given the law.' "

And yet rhythm gives to stage speech exceptional power and expressiveness. Again I cite here a quotation from Coquelin, since I think that everyone should study his small but brilliant book *On the Art of the Actor:*[3]

> Prevôt tells laughingly how once when he was finishing a tirade by Hippolytus, which the public had followed holding its breath, his memory failed him during the last two lines. To slow down the speech and wait for the prompter was impossible. Lightning quick he made his decision. With sublime inspiration and without breaking rhythm he delivered two lines of Volapük,[4] which the public did not understand but which it topped by a burst of wild applause; to such degree had gesture, emphasis, all the *movement of speech* imparted clarity, eloquence and power to this improvised language.**

*Jean d'Udin, *Art and Gesture*, trans. S. Volkonsky.

**Italics mine.

Let me cite two examples which in my opinion demonstrate the strength and power of rhythm in stage speech. In 1919 Vasili Kamensky's *Stenka Razin* played in Moscow.[5] Alice Koonen played the role of the Persian princess Meiran. There was one place in her role where no one, even with the most passionate desire to do so, could understand a word. And yet few places in the entire play so genuinely engrossed the attention of the audience, which, moreover, was made up for the most part of the most unsophisticated and uneducated spectators. Here is the place:

> Ai Khyal bura ben
> Siverim size chok
> Ai Zalma
> Ai gurmyzh-dzhamanai, etc.

At first Kamensky tried to make believe that these were Persian words, but later he admitted that they were, upon his honor, nothing at all. Nevertheless, the audience devoured them avidly. Why? Undoubtedly because with respect to voice and diction they were masterfully incorporated into the rhythm and vocal pattern of the character.

In *Famira Kifared,* by general admission, the best place was the scene in which Famira has the following stanzas, and it also was undoubtedly the most unintelligible so far as the text was concerned:

> Long have I watched Admet's herds,
> Admet's herds.
> O, delirium.
> Are you, Kifared, one who
> Abandons your friends?
> O, delirium
> Having tuned the flute,
> Invest it with
> Your own lustre.

I'll warrant you do not understand any of it (for I doubt you are familiar with the little-known myth of Admet, etc.) just as the majority of the audience understood nothing. But the rhythm of the lines was worked out so happily that the audience listened in rapt attention to Zeretelli, who delivered them.

The fascination of rhythmic speech is gradually coming to be understood by the spectator and even, *horribile dictu,* by critics. Not so long ago, when Alice Koonen, who is extraordinarily successful in this regard, was playing the role of Minerva in *The Azure Carpet,* there was no end to the criticism of the "unnaturalness" of her speech. Now, in *Adrienne Lecouvreur,* when her delivery is markedly more daring, the same critics find it beautiful.

It's about time!

Along with the rhythmic principle in stage speech, one must include the principle of dynamics. Speech, like gesture, must be effectual; it must be ordered according to its own aims, objects, aspirations. Only then will it receive its necessary emphasis and expressiveness. Also, the actor's voice must be free, but of course not unpredictable. I do not speak about the fact that it (as well as breathing) must be finely developed and cultivated. Nor do I mention that the actor must have faultless diction. These, according to the apt definition of Coquelin, are matters of "common civility on the part of the actor" and may be taken for granted. But, having developed his voice and knowing how to control it, the actor must not be afraid of it. Rather, he must use it freely and generously in the creation of the stage figure, since sound is without doubt one of the most important means for the transmission of the actor's intent to the audience. The actor's voice must change from *piano* to *forte,* from conversation to singing, from *staccato* to *legato* in harmony with and dependent on his creative demands. And do not worry about its being "unnatural" so long as it is justified by your character, as it was in those stanzas of *Famira Kifared* when Famira's voice rang out first in speech, then rose into song, then again in speech, or, in the same play, in the monologue of the Nymphs.

"As the role varies so does the timbre, key and tonality of the actor's voice," says Coquelin.

"There is, it seems, a chromatic scale," says Madelon. To find the necessary key and scale for every character, that is the task which faces the new actor. Only when he has mastered perfectly internal and external technique will the actor become a genuine artist, a master of his art. And then all those attempts to bury the theatre, in the name of literature such as Eichenwald's, or in the name of the super-marionette such as Craig's, will disappear once and for all.

The super-actor will gaily guard its entrances, creating within it his beautiful, self-contained theatrical art.

V.

The Director

The art of the theatre is the art of action. It is realized on the stage by "one who performs an action," i.e., an actor, who is thus the sole and sovereign bearer of theatrical art.

This being the case, what is the role of the director in the theatre? What need is there of him? What do his duties consist of?

The art of the theatre is a collective art. Scenic action appears as a result of the very collisions that occur in its process; it is a result of the interrelations and conflicts which take place between individual "ones who act" or groups of them. In order that these conflicts not be governed by chance, in order that the scenic action be not chaotic but flow in orderly fashion, that it be cast not in separate and uncoordinated but in harmonious forms which follow one after another in a unified work of theatrical art, it is obvious that *someone* is needed. There must be someone who, creatively striving for this result, regulates and directs the conflicts that arise—softening, strengthening, eliminating, creating—in order to lead all the action to its harmonious completion.

This "someone" is the *director*.

Insofar as the theatre is a product of collective creativity, it requires a director, whose intrinsic role is the coordination and ultimate harmonization of the creativity of the separate individualities.

So it is, always has been, and always will be.

Under various guises, under various names, the director has invariably existed in the theatre; and he will continue to exist because he was engendered by the very essence of theatre art—its basis in action and the collective nature of its creativity. The director is the helmsman of the theatre; he pilots the ship of the theatrical production, avoiding shoals and reefs, surmounting unexpected obstacles, wrestling with storms and gales, unfurling and trimming the sails, and all the time guiding the ship toward a predetermined creative goal.

Insofar as the director is the pilot of the theatre, he undoubtedly limits to some degree the freedom of all the separate "ones who perform an action" in it.

Having proclaimed the invariable primacy of the actor, his hegemony in the theatre, having accounted him the sole and sovereign bearer of theatrical art, it would seem that now I am contradicting myself. But this is only a seeming contradiction. We need only look more carefully into the relationship between the director and actor to be convinced that in this case the dependence of the actor is in essence the strongest possible affirmation of his creative freedom.

I have no wish to play with words, and I am not inclined to paradox, but the structure of the theatre is such that there cannot be freedom for the actor outside this dependence.

You see, the theatre is indeed a collective art. The completely unrestrained creative freedom of a given individual will of necessity either neutralize the freedom of other individuals who come in contact with him during the action, or will transform the generated conflict from a factor which creates action to one which destroys it. In order that the individual freedom of every "one who performs an action" may be realized to the maximum—without detriment to the creatively directed wills of those other individuals who come in contact with him in the course of the action—it is necessary that there be some voluntary self-restraint and subjugation to the director. All concerned must depend on his talent and creative sensitivity to turn this act of voluntary self-restraint into a new assertion of the actor's freedom.

Naturally it is necessary that the director who takes unto himself such a tremendous and responsible mission be worthy of it, that he be a genuine master of the stage. In this new theatre about which I speak it may not be otherwise. Is it likely that a genuine master-actor, an actor who commands all the means and secrets of his art, would permit an untrustworthy pilot to stand at the helm of his ship?

So, I maintain that the art of the director is an integral part of the art of the theatre, and that in his intended capacity he not only does not restrict but rather assures the freedom of the individual actor's creativity.

Why, then, is the life of the contemporary theatre full of censures and complaints against the suppression of the actor's creativity by the director?

Why do we hear that the director has turned the theatre into some kind of Procrustean bed, where the actor's creative ego is hemmed in, and where the actor cannot find for himself a full and joyful means of expression? These reproaches are made and in large measure justified not because the role of the director is in its essence that of suppressor of the actor's creative ideas, talent, and freedom, nor even because the majority of contemporary directors are so incompetent that they really have no right even to get near a theatre—but because *those scenic trends which have been cultivated by the most prominent directors of our time have placed them in a position where, like it or not, they must suppress the actor.*

I have already had occasion to say more than once that the contemporary theatre has developed along the lines of naturalism and stylization. Owing to separate causes inherent in each of these trends, the directors of both schools were deprived of the possibility to give free rein to the actor's creativity.

You know that the naturalistic theatre regards the principle of verisimilitude as of paramount importance; a play must evoke in the spectator the illusion of real life and not a stage production. Guided by this principle, the director had of necessity to secure from the actor a performance which would give the audience the impression that he was Ivan Ivanovich, Maria Ivanovna—a person taken as it were right out of life. In achieving this, he was forced to restrain the actor and to deprive his creativity of its color. In order not to destroy the illusion of life, he had to curtail the actor's gesture, muffle his voice, make his speech a-rhythmic, etc., that is, he had to deprive the actor of the possibility of using those means of expression, that material by means of which only he could create his art. For as soon as the actor was given the possibility of using his material, then his first genuine gesture, the first freely born sound of his voice, would at once smash to smithereens the whole structure of verisimilitude being constructed with such difficulty, and the spectator's illusion would come tumbling down.

Therefore, the director of the naturalistic theatre, however gifted and skillful, had *of necessity to stifle* genuine acting creativity. The evil in this case was inevitable; it arose as a logical and inexorable consequence. For once the director let himself be guided by a false principle, one fundamentally alien to theatre art, he had also to subjugate the actor to this false principle, thereby entering into actual conflict with genuine acting creativity and suppressing it.

From this point of view, and within the limits of this particular school of theatre, the resultant criticisms concerning the dominance of the director were undoubtedly well-founded.

The director of the stylized theatre fell into the same situation, albeit in a different way. Having given the position of utmost prominence in his work to style, and striving accordingly to suppress the actor's real being, which serves as his material, trying to force the real forms of the actor's creativity into a stylized design—trying to stylize his emotions, as it were—the director of the stylized theatre, just as the director of the naturalistic one, was faced with the necessity of denying the actor creative use of his own material. For if by using his material in the naturalistic theatre the actor would destroy the illusory structure of life, in the stylized theatre he would by the same token destroy the just as illusory structure of non-life—that whole mechanized structure to which, as we have seen, that theatre inevitably came.

Thus here too, in the stylized theatre, the director subjugated the actor to a false principle, fundamentally alien to art, and therefore had *of necessity to suppress* him—thereby justifying the widespread opinion that the director was dominant, and that he was inevitably so.

As a matter of fact, this dominance is not at all an organic part of the role played by the director in the theatre; it is only a consequence of the indicated schools, for which certain directors have acted as champions. The falsity of the director's position was brought about not by the falsity of the phenomenon of the director in general, but by the falsity of the trends these directors set in motion.

Therefore, it is of course absurd to infer that the director generally is an abnormal phenomenon in the theatre, that he will inevitably suppress the actor's creativity, that with the renaissance and development of the theatre he is doomed to degenerate or even disappear. And of course Valery Briusov is just as wrong when he says that the director in the theatre is no more, as it were, than the editor of a journal.

No. The role of the director in the theatre is a tremendous one, and the more the theatre follows the path of its own perfection and self-expression, the more significant that role will become, for then the director will embody in himself the playwright as well, creating and bringing to life a given scenario with the help of the acting collective.

However, there is at present a theatre in which we do not hear the fashionable criticism of directorial dominance,* in spite of the fact that the role of the director is most active there, so active that it almost approaches the degree I have just mentioned. I am speaking of the ballet.

If you look closely into the art of the ballet and into the sort of role the

*If the director is talented, of course.

ballet master plays in it, at first glance it seems as though the director is much
more despotic here than in any other theatre, that he oppresses the actor to a
much greater degree than any of the others. In fact, the ballet master, in his
work with the actors, determines the entire pattern of the role down to the
smallest details. It is not just that this or the other basic movement of the
ballerina is provided for, nor even her every *pas,* but every turn of her head,
every movement of her arms and hands, sometimes even her little finger—and
nevertheless, I have never had occasion to hear complaints about the "domina-
tion" of the director.

This comes about because in the ballet the essence of its art is less obstruc-
ted by attendant elements than in any other theatre; because here the action-
essence of the theatre has been preserved in its most pure form; because having
been trained in the same school—which gives to acting mastery the tremendous
significance it deserves—the ballet master and the actor understand each other
to the fullest.

The actors and actresses of the ballet know that the pattern established together with the ballet master not only does not deprive them of the opportunity to express their own individual creativity, but on the contrary opens to
them this very possibility. This is true because the final form which is the result
of all the bits of work imposed or approved by the ballet master is based on a
strict accounting of all the individual capacities of the given actor, in connection with the general creative plan of the whole production. Constructed in
this fashion, the form not only does not restrict him, but on the contrary gives
him indispensible confidence that the emotion he develops will not overwhelm
him but will be cast in precisely those shapes which will communicate his art
to the audience with the greatest strength, precision, and joy.

Unfortunately, formalism and some other phenomena which I have already
mentioned are now destroying this interdependence of actors and the director
in ballet. But this is essentially how it must be on every stage which sets its
foot upon the true path to theatrical art.

If the theatre stands firmly on a base of scenic action, if it does not subjugate itself either to naturalism or to stylization, if it does not fall under the influence of either literature or painting, if its whole and only intent is the maximum expression of the actor's creative will and the full-valued sounding of all
his material, if by these means, that is, by his own independent art, the actor
seeks to attract and win over his audience—in such a theatre there can be no
question of any kind of directorial despotism. In such a theatre the director's

whole task will be to help the actor find that scenic form, to give him that firm base, upon which, having become a full-fledged master, he can with ease display all the wealth of his creative potential. For it is only in the play of creativity's jewel-like facets that one may see all the charm, all the joy, and all the power of genuine theatrical action.

The art of the director is expressed primarily in the production process. This process may be broken down into several basic periods, the first of which, in my view, is the creative design of the production.

Genuine theatrical action hovers invariably between two basic poles—the *mystery* and the *harlequinade.* But between these poles it assumes special, original, and unique forms in every play, in every production. The first task of the director is to find a form for the production, taking into account the creative collective of the theatre, its strengths and needs, and that urge to action which lies in its path at that moment. Only when one has become aware of this urge and converted it to use may he set about the creation or interpretation of a scenario or play.

VI.   The Role of Literature
in the Theatre

We know that periods of flowering in the theatre have ensued when the theatre departed from written plays and created its own scenarios. Undoubtedly that theatre of our own hopes and aspirations, which we are working to bring into existence, sooner or later will also come to the same thing.

There are already indications of this in experiments which we are conducting and which I will discuss later. But in order that the theatre may create and mount its own scenarios, a new master-actor must be born who is in complete command of his art, for then the whole center of gravity will be transferred to him and to his independent mastery. It is vital that the whole acting collective consist of super-actors, masters, welded together by a single school and creatively united by one theatrical culture.

Of course the creation of such a theatre, a collective of such high capacity, is not the work of a few days, perhaps not even of a few years, but a generation. Naturally it is possible that this process will be completed sooner; it is difficult to estimate accurately how long it will take. But one thing is certain: it will be completed not in the hush of laboratory and studio investigations but in the active ferment of the living theatre, in the sacrificial fire—in which, and only in which, all the old clichés and traditions can be melted down and molded into new creative forms.

Since this is so, since "the play must go on," it is necessary to find for the time being temporary expedients and to employ them in such fashion that we approach ever closer to the projected goal. If at the present moment the theatre is not yet ready to reject written plays completely, then it must take them, using them in ways conformable to the task before it.

So, the theatre looks upon *literature* only as *material* necessary to it at the present stage of its development. Only such an approach to literature is genuinely theatrical, since otherwise the theatre will inevitably cease to exist as an art to be valued in and of itself, and will turn into a mere good or bad tributary of literature, a phonograph record, reproducing the ideas of the author.

You know it is considered the highest praise to say to a director: "How correctly you interpreted Shakespeare," or, "It is amazing how faithfully you reproduced Molière." You may think what you like, but for me such praise would sound like a funeral march. And Gordon Craig is profoundly wrong when in his first dialogue he answers a question concerning the director's role in the theatre with the following words: "What is his function? I will tell you. His job as *interpreter of the playwright's work* is something like this: He takes a copy of the play from the hands of the playwright and promises *to interpret it faithfully*, according to the instructions of the text."*

Is this really the purpose of the theatre? Does it really consist of giving the play a "faithful interpretation"?

No. The theatre's mission is enormous and autonomous. In mounting a play it must, in accord with its own artistic intention, its own urge to action, create *its own, new work of art to be valued in and of itself.*

In the last analysis, is not this the way all genuine artists have proceeded who believe in the power of their own art? Is not this the way all the best playwrights have worked, taking as material for their own work popular myths and legends of antiquity or stories from the holy scriptures created by unknown poets? And has this lessened the artistic value of their work; or has it provoked vindications such as Craig gives when he says that he wishes to remove plays from the stage because "it is my opinion that these plays are being distorted by the theatre? "**

From that point of view did not Shakespeare, the great Shakespeare, "distort" the Italian novella which had been reworked by Brooke as he created *Romeo and Juliet*? If you compare the texts of the novella and the tragedy, you will see that Shakespeare borrowed everything— the events, the order of their occurrence, the place of action, even names. But Shakespeare "distorted"

*Italics mine.

**Craig suggests that it is not only bad theatre which perverts plays but theatre in general, because it is invariably powerless to mount them properly, i.e., not to pervert them. As an example he cites one of the monologues of Macbeth, suggesting that "when art is so great and so perfect that it may by reading alone give us such magical values, then it is almost sacrilege to disrupt that which evokes these thoughts, confusing these feelings with the simultaneous appeal to other emotions, i.e., to view the play on stage."

all this—that is, he transformed it in his playwright's creative fantasy—and a *new*, beautiful dramatic work was born into the world.

Similarly, it is only after such a process of "distortion," i.e., transformation in the creative fire of the theatre, that a new *scenic* work may be born.

No, no genuine art may distort another. And every art, so long as it be genuine, is secure in its beauty.

But if Gordon Craig is wrong, that other "theatrical revolutionary" Vsevelod Meyerhold is saying simply monstrous things. In the article to which I have already referred, he writes: *"A new theatre grows out of literature. Literature always takes the initiative in the breaking of dramatic forms. Literature creates theatre."**

Always?

Was Meyerhold's beloved commedia dell'arte also created by literature? Or Molière, who really did create a theatre with his own literature (his plays), was he himself not in turn influenced to a significant degree by Scaramouche and his troupe? Here is what Louis Moland writes of Molière:**

> During the time the Italians were playing, Molière was imprisoned for his debts, and when he was released, he fled Paris. Returning in 1658, he again met with Scaramouche and his troupe, and they shared the Petit Bourbon, where Molière's productions played four times a week and the Italians' three. The two troupes were very friendly. Molière, who was thirty-six at the time and in the flower of his talent, borrowed much from the famous Italian actors. His enemies reproached him for it. Villier writes of Molière:"If you wish to play Elomire well, picture a man in whom are mixed elements of Harlequin, Scaramouche, the Doctor, Trivelin. Let Scaramouche claim his walk, his beard and his grimaces, and let the others claim what was taken from them—from their costumes and actions."

And was not the literature of Goldoni himself engendered to a significant degree by the theatre of commedia dell'arte? How can one say after this that literature creates theatre?

But perhaps Meyerhold's words refer only to the contemporary theatre. In that case he is undoubtedly right in part, for, as I have already said, the naturalistic theatre was in complete bondage to literature; nor, judging from the statements of Meyerhold, was the stylized theatre free from this captivity

---

*I cite Meyerhold from this particular article because all his subsequent work, theatrical as well as literary, introduces nothing essentially new or important. From here on he only repeats himself.

**La vie de Scaramouche.

(Maeterlinck, Ibsen, etc.). But then neither the naturalistic nor the stylized was genuine theatre, cultivating its own self-contained art. Perhaps they were not such precisely because they were created by literature. That is not to say, however, that the literature by which they were created has in itself no right to the theatre.

In the Roman theatre during the time of Livius Andronicus there was a custom according to which a single role was often performed simultaneously by two actors—a mime and a reader. In this way, through pantomime, they tested as it were the play's potential for scenic action and the consequent suitability of the play for the theatre.

Of course neither Chekhov, who created a whole epoch in the naturalistic theatre, nor Maeterlinck, who, according to the authoritative acknowledgment of Meyerhold, created in large measure the stylized theatre, would withstand such a trial by the active fire of the theatre.

How then could they have "created" a theatre!

No, the institutions created by them were not and could not have been genuine theatres.

That genuine new theatre toward which we are now moving and to which I am constantly referring here *will of course be created not by literature but by a new master-actor,* who even now, even in the first steps of his development, finds himself cramped by the limits imposed on him by literature.

In the process of our development we already have found it necessary to seek for ourselves material *outside* existing dramatic literature, for its forms often turn out to be too confining for our scenic constructions. This explains our turning to non-dramatic literature, and particularly to Hoffmann. We are guided in this case not by the desire to stage Hoffmann, "to interpret him faithfully," but by the desire to avoid dealing with ready-made scenic forms which only restrict us.

You see, there are no plays in existing dramatic literature answerable to the purposes of a synthetic scenic construction—one which would fuse the now separated elements of the Harlequinade, tragedy, operetta, pantomime, and circus, refracting them through the modern soul of the actor and the creative rhythm kindred to it (Gozzi proved too primitive for this purpose). Therefore, we ourselves create them, using Hoffmann, for in his unbridled fantasy we find rich material, rhythmically consonant with our scenic aspirations. But in "distorting" Hoffmann, i.e., in scenically transforming him, we create much ourselves, using our own creative capacity as a base, and in this way

draw nearer to our final goal, the independent creation of the whole production. That is why we named our production of *Princess Brambilla* a *capriccio*
of the Kamerny Theatre.

However, I must make a reservation. I think that even in the future, when
we have reached our goal, we will still need a helpmate for the creation of our
plays. Here again I cannot agree with Gordon Craig, who thinks that the trou-
ble with the contemporary theatre is that there is no single person "who might
be the complete master, that is, there is no person capable of writing and re-
hearsing a play, capable of designing and supervising the construction of sets
and costumes, capable of writing notable music, or inventing the necessary
machines and appropriate lighting."

In my view that is not a misfortune but a piece of luck for the theatre,
since of course such a person could not be a *master* in any case. To learn everything enumerated by Craig well enough to be a master in all the designated
areas is not within the power of one man. However gifted he might be, human
life is not long enough. That means that such a man would inevitably be a
dilettante—talented perhaps, perhaps even brilliant, but nevertheless a dilettante, i.e., *a person incapable of creating anything.* He will never be the builder
of a theatre. At the best he will be a theoretician or a critic or a more or less
inspired enthusiast.

Or he might in the end even turn out to be a person who strives to destroy
the theatre.

You see, to be consistent in the extreme, this new theatrical messiah must
certainly be an actor also, an actor moreover who plays *all* the roles, for otherwise the theatre would not have that "unity" about the lack of which Craig
complains.* Only under such a condition can that "theatre of one will" about
which F. Sologub also dreams be created.

But then this also is the direct route to the destruction of the theatre, to
the banishment of the actor and to his replacement by the marionette. Alas,
that dilettante-master after which Craig pines leads directly to the *"über-
marionette."*

No, the theatre is a collective art and it must be accepted as such. Unity,
without which of course any work of art is unthinkable, is born as the result
of the marriage of a whole line of wills, merging at last into a single, monolithic work of scenic art.

*For the sake of "unity" it is undoubtedly much more important than designing sets
or inventing machines.

The overseer of this process, who as it were concentrates in himself the creative will of the whole collective, is the *director,* who in this area must undoubtedly be a genuine and inspired *master.* Then he need not fear the *helpmates* necessary to him. However experienced masters, each in his own area, they may be, they will not drag him about like some "monstrous Leviathan." On the contrary, he himself will easily lead them after him if only he is in truth a master, if he declares allegiance to the genuine art of the theatre—the art of theatrical action –and truly masters it.

It is the *poet* who must be the helpmate to the theatre in the creation of the play. For it is given only to him, his gift and mastery, to invest the actor's speech with the necessary rhythmic pattern and give it a finished artistic form in those moments of scenic action when the pathos of a given emotion demands it.

I dare say it has almost always been so, that almost always the poet has been the unfailing helpmate of the actor and the theatre. One may find corroboration of this view in the extremely curious investigations of Richard Pichel:*

> The Indian drama presents itself to us in its most finished form in the plays of Kalidasa (sixth century B.C.). The form of his dramas reveal the history as well as the technique of Indian drama. The hymns in the dialogues of the Rigveda and in other works such as the Suparnodhyaya are completely unintelligible in the form in which they have come down to us. The connection between separate verses is very weak; often it is impossible to find. To understand them we need a connecting text, which in some cases is given in the prose of the Brahmanas and in explanatory pages in the Vedas.
>
> The later works also, such as the Mahabharata and Puranas, sometimes contain a whole story, but often in very different form. Windisch, in examining similar occurrences in Irish literature, concluded that only the verse passages of the original were permanent and that the narrators connected them with prose at their own discretion. This point of view is undoubtedly correct. It is confirmed also by the name for the rhapsodists—*granthika*—"the one who connects." The detailed working out of the prose connection between the verses is given over entirely to the talents of the rhapsodist. So it was originally with the drama in India. The classical drama in India is constructed in such a way that the prose is invariably interrupted by verse stanzas of various meters. In *pre-classical* times such stanzas comprised *the only inviolable element of the drama. With respect to the prose the artist was given complete freedom.*** This situation has been preserved to the present in folk plays.

The Home of the Puppet Play.
**Italics mine.

If this interesting research once again confirms that *the theatre and actor can themselves freely create their own art without written dramas,* it also gives on the other hand an irrefutable indication that in the period of the theatre's flower, when the actors themselves created both the acting scenario and the speech necessary for its embodiment, they were nevertheless aided by the *poet,* who shaped their speech into stanzas of verse when it was demanded by the swelling pathos of their emotions.

And of course this did not at all deprive the work of theatrical art, which they were creating, of its "unity." On the contrary, so long as the actor did not lose his mastery and the poet did not turn into a playwright, the help of the poet undoubtedly enriched the art of the actor with a new and beautiful facet —the mastery of rhythmic speech.

In the work of the Kamerny Theatre we are at present conducting an experiment with such collaboration on the part of the poet in the theatre's active creation of its own plays, and it may very well be that yet this season this construction will be confirmed by the only authoritative judge in all creative questions—a living theatrical performance.

So, the discovery of the literary material necessary for the selected scenic project, and its transformation into a correspondingly effectual production structure—this is the second step of the creative process in the director's creation of the production.

VII.

Music in the Theatre

The next—and perhaps no less important—stage in the director's preparatory work is the stage I choose to call the orchestration of the play and the solution of its rhythm.

It is long past time that we stopped looking upon the verbal material the theatre uses as just so many words expressing this or that idea or thought. It is time at last that we begin to look on it as we do pantomimic material, from the point of view of the rhythm contained in it and the harmonic and phonetic possibilities which a given piece of verbal material presents.

To become aware of the rhythmic beat of a play, to hear its sound, its harmony, and afterwards as it were to orchestrate it—that is the third task of the director.

I have long felt the need for such an approach to the verbal material of a production, but I felt it especially strongly and undeniably in working on the production of *Salome*. [1] The rhythmic and contrapuntal pattern beats so clearly in its verbal material and appeals so irresistibly for fulfillment, that so far as I am concerned it is absolutely impossible to pass by. And in fact the work of exposing and then realizing the pattern and orchestrating the whole work (the contra-basses of the soldiers, the flute of the young Syrian, the oboe of Salome, the sounding brass of Jochanaan, etc.) occupied a significant place in our production.

Work of a similar kind played perhaps no less significant a role in *Famira Kifared*, where, as I have already pointed out, in places the speech bridged over spontaneously into singing. I also constructed the production of *Princess Brambilla* to a significant degree on the rhythmic bases of the Tarentella and Saltorella.

The great significance of all these elements in the work of the theatre un-questionably relates it very closely to music.

Of all the arts, music assuredly is the closest to the theatre.

Even the ancient Hellenes perceived this relationship, giving the gods of music and dance (i.e., gesture, meaning theatre as well) names stemming from one and the same root: Euterpe and Terpsichore. Even the masterful Gluck felt this when, in composing Orpheus, he placed chairs about the room to re-present the dramatis personae, and before finally writing down the melodies which had formed in his head, staged them as it were to test their acting po-tential. Jean d'Udin demonstrates this brilliantly in his excellent book.

All of us working to solve the problem of rhythm in the theatre feel its relation to music keenly, and our work on the pantomime convinced us of its closeness beyond the shadow of a doubt. My work on the production of The Demon also convinced me, as I constructed the entire mise-en-scène—the movement of individual characters as well as all of the choral scenes—to an exceptional degree on a rhythmic base. [2]

Just as the theatre needs the poet as a creative helpmate, so also it needs the composer in order that the self-contained art of the theatre may begin to express itself with all the inexhaustible plenitude of its many-faceted poten-tialities, so that the creative palette of the actor may begin to sparkle with new and vibrant colors.

I can affirm this now with all that joyful confidence given me by joint the-atrical work with Henri Forterre for a period of over four years. The Marriage of Figaro, Famira Kifared, King Harlequin, and Princess Brambilla—these are the inspiring witnesses to what beautiful colors the composer who keenly sen-ses and creatively assimilates the active spirit of the theatre can give to the actor.

Such a composer, of course, cannot either "enslave" the actor or, on the other hand, "abase" his music by subjugation to the theatre. Gluck was not afraid of abasing his music by "staging" Orpheus. And if in Famira Kifared the bacchanal scenes were set to music before they were staged, in Princess Bram-billa, on the contrary, the entire pantomime of the second act, lasting fifteen minutes, was worked out on the stage first and afterward found its harmonic and rhythmic completion in music.

The theatre is just now taking its first steps in its work on rhythm, and yet already one senses how beautiful is that new power which it imparts to the creativity of the actor. In the future this work will expose exceptionally exciting possibilities to the theatre. I speak of that time when the theatre and actor so master rhythm that they may carry out on the stage a plan of action not only in rhythm with the musical design but a-rhythmically as well, but in such fashion that it is musically regular in itself. That new visual-auditory harmony which will be born of this process will undoubtedly give us still unexplored creative joys.

Then perhaps will appear the wonderful possibility for the construction of genuine theatrical mystery, when triumph and despair, revolution and tranquillity, happiness and grief are woven into a single circle of alternating action and when their uncoordinated rhythms will give birth to a new and startling harmony.

VIII.
Scenic Atmosphere

The final period in the director's preparatory work is devoted to working out the necessary place of action for a given production, i.e., that scenic atmosphere in which the actor must function. Naturally this task is of paramount importance, because a given scenic atmosphere may either aid the actor greatly in realizing his creative intent or, on the contrary, categorically obstruct him, almost actively preventing the realization of his plans.

Of course the problem of scenic atmosphere is not a new one; the actor has never been able to perform in a vacuum. Consequently there has always arisen a need to find some base or other suitable for the development of the action he is bringing to life. In antiquity the arena of the amphitheatre served as such a base, in the middle ages the steps, facades, and interiors of cathedrals or the scaffold stages of fairs, in our times the stage house of theatres. By the same token, every period solved the problem of scenic atmosphere in its own way, and even in the same period this problem found different, often diametrically opposed solutions—depending upon what principles lay at the base of a given theatre or a given theatrical trend.

If we trace the history of the development of scenic atmosphere during that period of the contemporary theatre I have been discussing, we may describe its evolution briefly as follows: *from model through sketch to neo-model.* In this evolution the director has invariably been accompanied and aided by the artist.

It is not surprising that in creating that atmosphere in which its actor was obliged to live, the naturalistic theatre sought the necessary solution in a *model.* Pursuing the goal of truth to life, the naturalistic theatre had of course to place its actor in such surroundings as would allow both the audience and the actor himself to give themselves up body and soul to the deception being created by the theatre and to believe that they were dealing not with the stage but with real life. In order that the actor be true to life in his emotional "experiencing," it was necessary that the surrounding scenic atmosphere give him in its turn that illusion of life without which it would be difficult for him to feel himself in an atmosphere approximating that of everyday.

With this goal, as I have already had occasion to point out, they began to construct on stage first rooms, then a series of rooms, then whole apartments, and finally whole houses. To erect such unwieldy constructions on the stage straight off was, of course, impossible. First the scale, the plans, the perspectives, etc., etc.—all had to be tested in miniature; only then could everything be transferred to the stage without risk of making an error.

Nothing answered to the purpose of preparatory testing, experimenting, and checking so well as the scale model. Thus it was natural that the scale model became the distinctive assay office of the naturalistic theatre, confirming the "lifelikeness" of the scenery being scraped together for any given production.

The role of the artist in working out such a model was in essence very modest. I do not risk falling into great error even if I say that in the period of the naturalistic theatre's flower, the role of the artist was anti-artistic, because the theatre and its director placed before the artist not the task of this or that artistic composition but the creation of the illusion of living truth, the fundamental characteristic of which is haphazardness, which destroys any artistic composition at its source.

I dare say that in this case there is no need of examples. All this is still so fresh in our memory that proofs are not necessary, and it was all stated in frank and unvarnished fashion in the long-suffering model.

What then is so surprising in the fact that when the reaction against the naturalistic theatre arose, when the stylized theatre overthrew the principles of naturalism and proclaimed the principles of stylization, replacing the demand for living truth with the demand for artistic convention—that then the wrath and hatred of its directors and even more of its artists fell first of all upon the anti-artistic nature of the naturalistic theatre and the model which personified it?

But having correctly sensed and evaluated the theatrical illiteracy and artistic unacceptability of the naturalistic model, the artist and director of the stylized theatre decided that the error of the naturalistic theatre lay not in *how* it constructed the model but in the fact that it constructed it at all. The model had become as it were a symbol of the naturalistic theatre, and it seemed that in order to destroy this theatre it was necessary first of all to destroy the model. Meyerhold writes,

> When many models had been built, representing *intérieurs* and *extérieurs* just as they are in life [Why just as?! A.T.], the model shop suddenly became gloomy, touchy, ill-tempered, already waiting for the moment when someone would at last cry out that it was high time all models were crushed and burned up. Twisting the model round and round, we turned the contemporary theatre about in our hands. We wanted to trample and burn the models because we felt that in this way we could draw nearer to our goal of stamping out the obsolete methods of the naturalistic theatre.

You see, the destruction of the model became an ideological necessity for the stylized theatre.

Alas, neither the director nor the artist of the stylized theatre, trampling and burning models, realized that they were trampling and burning not only, as they intended, the "obsolete devices of the naturalistic theatre," but *theatre* as a whole also. For in destroying *not the incorrect principles behind the construction of the model but the model itself,* they destroyed at the same time that *three-dimensional scenic space* without which the actor cannot perform.

Declaring that "working on models is an intolerable occupation for artists," passing *from the model to the sketch,* the stylized theatre passed at the same time from three-dimensional space to *two-dimensional* space, dooming the three-dimensional actor to inevitable transformation into a flat marionette. Having saved the artist from the "intolerable occupation" of working on models, and having placed at his disposal the worthy art of sketching, the director of the stylized theatre unwittingly placed the theatre under the authority of the artist.

The artist, who had long pined for frescoes and great canvases, now, shifting to the sketch, avidly transferred to the stage his habitual methods of easel painting with its flat treatment of form, and introduced into this treatment the living figure of the actor, flattening him and spreading him out. And this, along with a whole raft of other causes about which I spoke earlier, led to the fatal mechanization of the actor and, as the logical completion of the whole stylized design of the theatre, to his replacement by the marionette.

In creating the Kamerny Theatre we felt a clear and immediate need to free ourselves from the stifling hegemony of the artist, to extricate the actor from that role of picturesque blemish into which he had fallen as a result, and to push back the decorative panels which had been moved up almost to the very footlights—freeing the actor in this way from the two-dimensional design which had flattened him out, and opening up to him the arena of the stage for the free revelation of his own, self-contained art.

Seeking the solution of scenic atmosphere necessary for our purposes, we resorted for quite a long time to a whole line of palliative measures, combining and reforming the sketch every way possible, until at last, with the production of *Famira Kifared*, I came to feel that so long as the sketch itself existed scenic atmosphere absolutely could not be achieved effectively. And just as the styl-ized theatre had to trample and burn the model in order to free itself from the bonds of naturalism, so we had to *tear up and destroy* the sketch in order to free ourselves from the bonds of stylism and return to the theatre its primor-dial dynamic essence.

With the production of *Famira Kifared* I came to feel once and for all the indispensability of constructing the production plan on a base of rhythmic action, the necessity of giving the actor maximum possibility for movement, of arranging in a fashion answerable to this need *the stage floor,* that funda-mental base upon which alone movement can practically be displayed.

Transferring in this way the center of attention in our search to the floor of the stage, I naturally returned to a consideration of all its three-dimensional characteristics and came inevitably once more to the model. But of course this was not the model of the naturalistic theatre, but that *neo-model* which was to serve me as a true compass in my search for genuine, dynamic, scenic atmosphere.

For the visible manifestation of his art, the actor uses his own material. This material is the actor's body. The body of the actor is *three-dimensional*; therefore, it can be properly incorporated and displayed only in a three-dimen-sional atmosphere. Such an atmosphere may be worked out only in a definite cubic capacity, and of course only the scale model can serve as a pattern for such a cubic capacity.

But what should this model be like? On what principles should it be constructed?

The actor displays his art with the help of his body. It follows that the stage must be so constructed as to help the body of the actor to assume the necessary forms, to respond easily to all the necessary tasks of rhythm and movement. Hence it is clear that the chief part of the stage to be worked out with every production must be the *stage floor,* the so-called scenic platform, because it is precisely upon this that the actor moves and translates his creative tasks into reality in a visible form. Therefore the scenic artist must transfer the center of his attention to the stage floor, diverting it from the back panels which hold such attraction for him.

Until now the artist has completely disregarded the stage floor, devoting all his generous fantasy to the backdrop, wings, drops, teasers, working them out with such care and splendor that one might think the stage were intended not for actors but for some kind of fantastic bird soaring about in the air. Therefore, the artist must at all costs be distracted from these parts of the stage, which play only an auxiliary role, and all his attention must be concentrated on working out the acting platform with the director.

How must this platform be treated? What are the guiding principles upon which its construction must be based?

First of all the stage floor must be broken up. It must not be a single flat plane but must be broken up—depending on the aims of the production—into a whole series of horizontal or sloping surfaces of varied heights. For a level floor is manifestly inexpressive; it presents no possibility for the revelation of spectacle in relief; it does not give the actor opportunity to display movement in the proper degree, to make full use of his material.

I assume that this is sufficiently clear in itself. But if one wished one could confirm this at any time. First execute the series of movements which one can perform on the level expanse of the floor. Then place on the floor even so much as a stool, using it as a new plane, as a second area for the development of your movement, and you will see how your gesture is enriched, how many new plastic possibilities open up to you. If you had in front of you a series of platforms of varying heights, your material would acquire absolutely inexhaustible possibilities for gesture and form.

Of course the naturalistic theatre had no need to work out the scenic platform in such a fashion, for in life all people walk honestly on the level floor, and those who suddenly take it into their heads to climb up on tables and chairs are put in the insane asylum.

True, the stylized theatre sometimes made use of a broken-up scenic platform, but did so quite by chance and more for decorative than for acting reasons, making little use of the opportunities which arose therefrom, since such a consideration could not as such enter into the basic aim of the decorative composition of the artist.

Unfortunately, such a treatment of the stage floor is never used by the ballet, even though it would seem that with its cultivation of acting material and its frequent employment of massed choruses of the corps-de-ballet, it might find there hitherto unknown and exceptional beauties. If one looks closely at the usual ballet production, one is inevitably presented with the following: a whole mass of people crowds the stage, and the audience can perceive the movement of only an insignificant part of the chorus, those in the first row (I am speaking of course not of solo but of production numbers). This occurs because all the rows beyond the first one of the corps-de-ballet are lost for the spectator; he does not see them and is not in a position to be impressed by their movement. Thus all the arrangements of the mass scenes in *La Bayadère* (Bolshoi Theatre), for instance, are lost. [1] There is no way that the joy-giving harmony of mass-movement can impress the audience, since its view is constantly cut off by the obstructive wall of the first row of dancers.

An entirely different impression could be achieved if the floor of the stage were broken up and if rows of levels of various heights were arranged in such a way that the masses distributed on them might give the viewer the opportunity of seeing not just the first row alone but the whole corps-de-ballet. Clearly, the basic impression of a given act or scene depends largely on the overall movement of the corps. In breaking up the stage floor (in such fashion, of course, as not to interfere with the development of the dance—which is easy enough to do) you, Messrs. ballet-masters and ballet-directors, will allow everyone performing on the stage the opportunity to contribute to that total impression which the spectator receives from a given scenic presentation.

But the example I have cited reveals only the external, technical significance of such a treatment of the scenic platform. There is, indeed, another side to the thesis I am advancing here, a side which is markedly more profound and important for the actor. I think it will become clear if we recognize that the principle which determines the structure of the scenic platform is *one of rhythm.*

I have already said that every scenic task, every production has its own rhythm. All work on the production finds itself dependent on the rhythmic design of the play, and the playing area, too, must be constructed according to this rhythmic design.

Suppose that you have decided to stage the descent of the Virgin Mother. How should you construct the stage in order to achieve a dynamic impression of the descent? It is clear that you will not achieve this impression on the flat surface of the stage floor itself. The floor must be broken up. A series of levels of varying heights must be constructed, representing something like an unending flight of stairs, gradually conducting the actress-Virgin down from on high.

But how should these stairs be constructed? What should be the relationships among the steps?

This decision depends entirely on your rhythmic intent. If you wish the spectator to receive the impression that the Virgin descends almost without touching the earth; if you wish to attach a solemn, liturgical character to the action of the descent, you will construct the steps so that the intervals between them are everywhere the same. They will correspond rhythmically to 1/4 or 1/8 time, in this way giving to the movement of the actress an even and uninterrupted, flowing rhythm, as a result of which the impression of a liturgical descent of the Virgin is created in the performance.

But suppose you change the goal; suppose you want, for instance, to stage a wild, fiery bacchanal in honor of Dionysos. In accord with the changed rhythmic goal, you would break up the stage so that the levels of various heights would be connected by various and multiformed rhythms. Thanks to these the bacchanalian movement and satyrical leaps, acquiring the varied and multiformed undulations peculiar to the whole structure, would create the requisite dynamic impression of the bacchanal.

In constructing the model for *Famira Kifared,* I was faced with two rhythmic tasks at the same time. On the one hand, it was necessary to create a structure for the bacchanalian and satyrical movements of the production, in the turbulent throes of which arose and ripened the woeful tragedy of Famira. The latter in its turn demanded for its plastic manifestation a completely different structure, in counterpoise to the Dionysian rhythm of the first, taking as its base a precise and smooth-flowing Apollonian rhythm.

The designer for this production was Alexandra Ekster, an artist who responded with exceptional sensitivity to my scenic intentions and who displayed an excellent feeling for the dynamic element of the theatre from her very first acquaintance with it.[2] Working together in trying to give the model the rhythmic structure I required, we devoted the whole central part of the background of the model to platforms which expressed the Apollonian rhythm throbbing in the figure of Famira. All the side scenes were occupied by forms which, heaped up around the basic rhythmic design of the center, pulsated with all the multiformity of rhythmic variation characteristic of the cult of Dionysos. In this way, those fatal conflicts between the two cults, which permeated the tragedy of *Famira Kifared,* were already inherent in the very structure of the model.

"Famira Kifared"

The satyrs carry off the menads in the bacchanal

Thus, the construction of the model, or more precisely the construction of its floor, must be based on the rhythmic intent of the given production.

But in breaking up the floor of the stage and, as I have said, taking as our base platforms of various heights, we crossed over at the same time from the sphere of horizontal construction to the sphere of the vertical. We sensed that there might often arise the need not only for vertical constructions which serve as a base for the actor's movement, but for others as well, which could play their own independent and essential role.

On what principle should their construction be based?

Vertical constructions primarily satisfy the demands of scale. They must impart to the figures of the actors whatever scale is necessary to the intentions of a production, facilitating in this way the impression received by the spectator.

Imagine that we are staging a mystery play, in which it is necessary that the actor appear to be lost in the chaos of the universe, that he seem to be only an insignificant atom, a grain of sand, cast out into the vastness of space. In order to give the actor the possibility of making such an impression, we must create such grandiose vertical structures that the figure of the actor seems insignificant and lost. If, on the other hand, in some Harlequinade or other, our goal is to emphasize the strength and power of the actor's figure, dominating with its flashing movement and energy all the planets which surround it, then the vertical structures must be worked out so that the figure gliding over them seems to belong to Gulliver. Thus, owing to the vertical structures, the figure of the actor must in the eyes of the spectator now diminish, now grow to whatever degree is necessary for the actor's full manifestation of his creative intent.

Horizontal and vertical structures create on the stage a series of forms. What should these forms be like?

I think there is no longer any need to say that all structures on the stage must be three-dimensional, because only then can they harmonize with the three-dimensional body of the actor. This is obvious. We are interested now in another question: What should those *three-dimensional* forms, which obviously comprise the basic material in constructing the neo-model, be like? After all, *three-dimensional* forms often appeared on the stage in the naturalistic theatre —trees, stoves, hillocks, sometimes whole cliffs of papier-mâché, etc. Have we now in the end returned to them? And if not, then in what way do the three-dimensional forms of our new model differ from the three-dimensional forms of the naturalistic theatre?

The chief and most striking difference between them is that the forms of the naturalistic theatre are haphazard and pursue an independent goal—an anti-artistic one, moreover, namely, to create on the stage the illusion of life, while the three-dimensional forms of the neo-model are harmoniously regulated and arise not for the sake of creating a living or some other illusion, but solely to provide that indispensable rhythmic and plastic base for the actor's display of his art.

I think there is no further need for me to prove that by virtue of the fundamental principle which it professed, the naturalistic theatre transferred onto the stage the haphazard objects and forms of life, thereby invariably placing them outside the sphere of any kind of art. Even in placing on the stage realistically-styled furniture which in itself was executed with undoubted art, the naturalistic theatre still did not escape the manifest artistic contradiction between everyday "Empire" and the made-up face of the actor, however "lifelike." Not to mention the fact that every production, like any other work of art, must create its own complete world anew, and that even "Empire," created for a *given production,* must be different from any created for itself alone, by however fine a master. For with respect to a given production, so long as it aspires to genuine artistic originality, the latter will turn out haphazard notwithstanding. In this sense the multifarious forms representing hillocks, peaks, and mountains will be still more haphazard on the stage, however exactly and faithfully they copy the independently existing from of Elbrus, Kazbek, or some spur or other of the Pyrenees.

Art does not imitate nature.

It creates its own.

"I recognize no truth," says Gauguin, "but the truth of artistic falsehood."

It is not our concern that with the passage of many centuries, as a result of various atmospheric pressures and landslides, some mountain or other actually assumed a given form and no other. I, builder of the stage, penetrate within the phenomena I observe, and from the wondrous process of the universe take those primordial crystals in the creative harmony of which are concealed the joy and power of my art. These primordial crystals are those basic geometric forms which serve us as material in the construction of the new model.

Of course, these structures do not create any kind of lifelike illusion; they are, rather, truly free and creative constructions, recognizing no laws but the laws of internal harmony, engendered by the rhythmically dynamic structure of the production. From the point of view of verisimilitude, these structures may seem stylized. But in fact they are truly *real,* real from the point of view of theatre art, since they give the actor a real base for his action and harmonize perfectly with the reality of his material. It is also from this point of view that I call the new theatre *the theatre of neo-realism,* for it is created by the real art of the actor and, within the limits of theatrical truth, real scenic atmosphere.

But in suggesting that scenic structures be based on primordial geometric forms, am I not limiting the plastic possibilities of the stage, am I not condemning it to inexpressiveness, monotony, and boredom?

No, of course not.

Just as from three ciphers you can create a tremendous number of possible combinations, so from even three geometric forms are you free to create an inexhaustible series of the most diverse structures. If you take all the primordial forms and approach them not with the "consistency of a geometrician" but with the artist's freedom of creative transformation, then with all the generosity of your fantasy, you will still not find the limit to the harmonies arising ever new from them.

"But it is ugly," says the Philistine, shocked by the unaccustomed forms.

And is an automobile beautiful?

Remember, honorable Philistine, how it at first revolted your "aesthetic sensibility." Remember how absurd and deformed this new carriage seemed to you, with its blunt prow, lacking the usual horses in beautiful English harness, with its uncommon form, violating all our customary impressions. You agreed that it was comfortable and practical, only ugly. As if it could be compared with the beautiful equipage of a landau or a coach drawn by a pair of horses.

But only a few years passed and your "aesthetic" perception changed significantly: now you find great beauty in the automobile, that harmoniously complete, excellent equipage which transports you from place to place so swiftly and easily; and you gaze condescendingly and with some wonder at those strange monsters, those cumbersome carriages drawn by a pair of horses, which now only escort funeral processions, sadly, as if admitting their own obsolescence.

In such fashion did your notion of beauty evolve in only a short time. And if in constructing new forms even engineering revises your accustomed notions of beauty, then certainly art will not relinquish its own sacred and inherent right; art is of course even now undeterred by the fact that this or that form engendered by it turns out to be too much for the self-satisfied majority of aesthetically minded society.

We know very well that the public fears so-called "innovations" worse than anything in the world. Every new form invariably disturbs it, deprives it of that petit bourgeois security, that stagnant aesthetic comfort, in which it prefers to abide.

How is it possible not to treat such a phenomenon like an enemy?

But let some time pass, and the eye of the public becomes emancipated; that which earlier seemed ugly it now accepts as a new beauty, arming itself with its former bitterness against the next new form to be born in the unending creative process.

And still they say that the key to *perpetuum mobile* has yet to be found!

So I dare say we may quietly pass over the indignant cries against the "ugliness" of our structures in the firm conviction that already the moment is not far away when they will be accepted as the creators of a new beauty. Even now, although in all only four years have passed since the time when, in *Famira Kifared*, we first proved our structures on the stage, the cries of indignation which broke out at first are already beginning to subside. Meanwhile, the principles which we advanced are gradually finding echoes in the work of other theatres.

Just two years or so ago there was an attempt at a new scenic approach to the ballet (at the Aquarium Summer Theatre). As the performance began, from all corners of the parterre came the exclamation, "Why, that's the Kamerny Theatre." Not wishing to criticize in any way the work being carried out there, I must nevertheless insist emphatically that the superficial similarity caught by the public was exclusively external. Our structures seemed to me to be reflected as if in a warped mirror.

Later, in the New Theatre, directed by F. Komissarzhevsky, they played Shakespeare's *The Tempest*, the playing area of which unquestionably reminded one of the constructions of the Kamerny Theatre. But it, too, imitated only their external aspect, failing completely to uncover their much more significant dynamic essence. It was not molded around the rhythmic core of *The Tempest* and therefore remained always detached, alien to the actors performing on it. Whereas the playing area must be for the actor that flexible and obedient *keyboard* with the help of which he may express his creative will with the utmost completeness.

I will not point out the several other attempts to employ our structures which have taken place in other theatres; I will only say that of all of them, the young masters of the former Stroganov Academy came closest to the mark in this regard.* If you were at the exhibition of models arranged there in the spring of last year (notice—already models, not sketches), then you could easily have satisfied yourself that at least three-fourths of them, consciously or not, reflected the constructions of the Kamerny Theatre.

This may be explained in part by the fact that at the beginning of the school year I had occasion to give several talks there concerning the tasks of the artist in the new theatre. Maybe it is a result of the staff of instructors—artists who have worked in Kamerny Theatre productions. Maybe—and if this is so, so much the better—maybe it is simply that in the creative consciousness of the younger generation just such an approach to scenic atmosphere has developed of itself as the only thing consonant with the new theatrical conscience. But however it may be, this exhibition gave me great joy, since it was manifest evidence that the new artist dreaming about the theatre does not think like Meyerhold that "the pasting together of models is an intolerable occupation for artists." On the contrary, with the "neo-model" the new artist undoubtedly found the creative possibility to break free of the confining two-dimensional canvas and pass over to the exciting tasks of construction.

If you look at the canvases of the rayonists,[3] the cubists, and the futurists, you will easily understand that for them, too, and for a growing number of others of the new generation of artists, the construction of the new model is a genuine and interesting art. True, in crossing over to the new model, the artist is deprived of the possibility of transferring to the stage the principles of easel painting, which are alien to it. Nor may he transform the theatre into an exhibition hall for his pictures; but to make up for that he is presented with new and joyful tasks of rhythmic and plastic construction not bound by any laws but those of internal harmony and the dynamic composition of the production.

The principles which we discovered for the construction of the new model, while they are completely consonant with the genuine essence of theatrical art, nevertheless leave still unsolved one important aspect in the creation of scenic atmosphere. If you have ever been in the theatre during the so-called mounting rehearsals, or after the performance when in the weak illumination of the work lights the stage hands are dismantling the set, then you have no doubt experienced that somewhat strange, peculiar feeling which unconsciously and imperceptibly comes over us in those moments. You sit in the dark and empty

*Recently the influence of the scenic structures of the Kamerny Theatre has become noticeable even to the untrained eye in a whole line of theatres, even—horribile dictu—in the studios of the Art Theatre.

auditorium and look at the stage. Suddenly the backdrop which is hanging in front of you drops swiftly to the floor, and the undulating rays of ropes hang poised in mid-air. They interlace with other rays, trailing after the fallen backdrop. On the ghostly skeletons of the frames and on the toppled, now useless forms fantastic ships and masts rise up. Virgin, impenetrable forests fall to the ground, and secret, undulating corridors extend in endless windings and beckon to you.

The work continues.

In various places canvases and cloths float, now quietly, now soaring up with a rush, and in their capricious movement ever newer mirages loom up, powerfully drawing you into their orgiastic phantasmagoria.

O! This is theatre! you exclaim, joyfully excited by the unexpected explosion of the usually quiet and static scenic atmosphere. These are the invisible spirits of the theatre, which have brought to life by means of their own miraculous dynamism the dead and indifferent pieces of scenery. And you dream about a new, beautiful performance in which the dynamic elements of the theatre set to whirling about in their intoxicating dance not only actors but everything around them—when in the moments of the greatest accumulation of creative emotions, together with the actors' dynamic explosion into action, the entire scenic atmosphere begins to vibrate and change in harmonious, dynamic transformation, strengthening and saturating the beautiful mastery of the actor, afire in utmost self-revelation.

Imagine on the stage an actor, a hero who has raised an unquenchable mutiny against God. He abandons the earth in order to appear fearlessly before the face of the deity and cast a frenzied challenge into his teeth. Up a whole mountain of rising stage shapes he is drawn on. Now he reaches the final height —one daring flight now and the goal will be attained.

But this flight demands such a tremendous, superhuman gesture as even the most perfect master-actor cannot execute in all its fullness.

Then imagine that at precisely this moment, together with some kind of final gesture by the actor, stretching his expressiveness to its extreme limit, the whole scenic atmosphere rears up, resoundingly amplifying his gesture a thousand fold and fusing with him into a single, organic composition. And there before you is no longer a man but a powerful giant grown from the earth—forming, together with the whole structure engendered in the dynamic transformation, a single, monolithic figure, which you can believe will appear without fear even before the incinerating eye of The Almighty or of Fate.

In the production of *Salome* I took the first steps on the path to a solution of the *problems of dynamic transformation of scenic atmosphere.*[4] When, in a melody pregnant with action, suddenly, like an ominous warning, like the first call of inevitable doom, in the strident brass of Jochanaan's frenzied rhythm, a dark silver curtain opens before the spectator, revealing the fatal cistern, just as the golden gates open in the temple when the voice of the Lord is heard.

Further on, when the dynamic energy which has been accumulating in measure with the development of the action once more finds an outlet in Salome's sudden cry, "I will dance for you, Tetrarch," the greedy howl of joy which rips from the breast of Herod tears the backdrop asunder and carries it aside with waves of reverberating ether, revealing in the blood-drunk rays of the moon the red curtain of the dance and of death.

And now the Black Mass of moon and blood is completed, and the trembling Herod casts the ruthless shields of his soldiers upon Salome, senseless from the kiss of love and death, and merging with the swan song of the crushed princess, the black wings of the lowered banners vibrate in the air, a funereal canopy, abandoned by the moon, over the shield-tomb of Salome.

Unfortunately, this idea, beautifully worked out in the model, was not transferred to the stage with complete success for a whole raft of technical reasons. But even in the rudimentary form in which it had to be realized, it provides a foretaste of those exceptional joys which will come to light when the problem of dynamic scene changes is resolved in a genuine theatrical fact.

I think it necessary to emphasize that the dynamic changes about which I

"Salome"

"Salome": model by Alexandra Ekster

"Salome": the Sadducees; costume design by Alexandra Ekster

speak have nothing at all·in common with the so-called moving scenery to which the contemporary theatre sometimes has had recourse. I point this out because the moving scenery in Komissarzhevsky's production of *Tales of Hoffmann* was interpreted by the press as a further attempt to solve the problems I had raised.[5]

Of course, that is not so.

The movements of the scenery in *Tales of Hoffmann* were obviously pursuing the same goals as are pursued let us say in *Sleeping Beauty,* when strange shore lines pass before a stationary gondola as if it were moving, sailing past them.[6] The only difference is that in the ballet this is executed with the brilliant technical perfection peculiar to the craftsmanship of Valtz, whereas in the New Theatre it was done in an annoyingly amateurish fashion.[7] But in both instances movement has an independent, decorative, visual, one might say public-tour kind of goal. The director or designer plays guide, obligingly escorting the spectator to a new place of action. The center of attraction transfers from the actor and his art to the scenery. Instead of the actor's transporting the fantasy of the audience from one country to another by means of his own mastery of movement and gesture, he "freezes," and his active role is given over to moving scenery.

I am speaking about dynamic changes which play an auxiliary role with respect to the art of the actor, which act only as an accompaniment, setting off and vivifying his gesture, and which arise not from the demands of some change in landscape but out of that maximum emotional saturation which inevitably seeks a dynamic resolution.

Indeed, already at the beginning of the nineteenth century Hoffmann wrote: "Scenery must not attract the attention of the spectator as a splendid picture existing for itself alone. Rather, at the *instant of action* [italics mine] the spectator must feel unconsciously the influence of the picture in which the action is unfolding."*

Yes, *action,* as the basic element of the theatre, and not the *"place of* action" as some point or other on the immense globe of the world.

Theatre is theatre, not an atlas and not a movie travelogue, and *its only place of action is the stage* upon which the performance takes place. It is time to realize this with sufficient clarity to cease once and for all amusing the spectator with ethnographically motivated scenery.

The problem of dynamic changes which I have posed may be solved either

*Cited in Ignatov's book, *T. A. Hoffmann.*

with a whole series of technical contrivances or by the active participation of light in stage action. Unquestionably, we still do not value sufficiently the role of light on the stage, and the spirits which languish within the hermetically-sealed electric lamp have yet to be evoked. In our work on *Famira Kifared* we had the good fortune to come across a magician of light, who had mastered its wondrous secrets, by means of which, with the lavish willingness of the genuine artist, he wanted to enrich my work. I am speaking of the artist Salzmann.[8] The initial experiments which he conducted on the stage of the Kamerny Theatre, and afterwards the application of his amazing system to the model of *Famira Kifared,* presented us all with unforgettable moments. The stage house, the almost inevitable grave of many a quest, retired in mute impotence before the powerful torrent of light which saturated the model, and the walls disappeared, and the luminous atmosphere which poured forth changed color in response to the slightest pressure on the controlling lever.

Unfortunately, the war and the absence of necessary technical apparatus which it brought about, and the impossibility of ordering them from abroad prevented us from transferring Salzmann's system to the stage. What little we did succeed in doing with the means at hand in *Famira Kifared* was only a weak reflection of its radiance.* But I have not lost hope of reviving the interrupted experiments as soon as there appears any real possibility to do so. Then I believe that many things which are impossible for us now will become beautiful and joy-giving realities.

I have already said that in creating the scenic atmosphere necessary for the play the director is aided by the artist. Furthermore, as I think he himself has since become convinced, A. Lentulov was absolutely wrong when in one of his public debates on the theatre he said that I am driving the artist out of the theatre.[9] No, I am not driving him out at all. On the contrary, I am summoning his help, but in so doing I am setting him to different tasks than before. I want him to come to the stage for the glory of its one and only sovereign, the actor, not pushing him aside with his own art but, in creative collaboration with the director, creating that scenic atmosphere with the help of which the art of the actor may find and display itself in all its plentitude.

Such an atmosphere may be achieved only through the rhythmic structuring of the stage floor. Therefore, the theatre needs not the artist-painter but the artist-builder.

---

*With the revival of *Famira Kifared* in 1920, we had to deny ourselves even that little which had been accomplished earlier.

Saying that the artist of the new theatre must be a builder, I do not mean to say at the same time that he need inevitably be an architect. No, the artist of the new theatre may be an architect, or a painter, or a sculptor, if only he senses the elemental dynamism of the theatre and is drawn to realize it in a rhythmic and colorful construction. For the demands of this or that architectural style are alien to our goals, which are characterized by a striving after genuinely colorful compositions.

Color plays a significant and beautiful role on the stage. Though I do not wish to turn the stage into a picture gallery, I desire even less to deprive it of color, to rob it of color's expressive power, which is unquestionably capable of inspiring many striking moments in the actor as well as the spectator and of giving to the entire scenic atmosphere perfect artistic harmony. But just as scenic construction is founded on a rhythmic and plastic task, so the color of its composition must answer to the corresponding designs of a given production.

The color composition of *Famira Kifared,* for instance, was based on black, blue, and gold, saturating, as it were, the scenic atmosphere with the sun-bright striving of Famira after Apollo, which culminates in the dark tragedy of his blindness. On the other hand, the goals of color in the Harlequinade may impel the artist toward an entirely different composition, sparkling and variegated like the cloak of Harlequin *(King Harlequin* and *Princess Brambilla).* [10]

And so on, and so on.

Only one thing is important, that the color composition not conflict but rather harmonize with the basic intent of the production, at the same time adding to the art of the actor new expressiveness and clarity.

Even in deep antiquity the theatre understood color very well and attributed just such significance to it, as is evident from the quotation from the history of Indian theatre which I have already cited. Of course I am not at all offering our artists the recipes of ancient India. I desire only that we do not overlook the truth hidden there, freely refracting it through our sensitivity of a theatrical and artistic culture which has advanced a long way.

Besides the tasks already indicated, still one more no less significant task stands before the artist.

I am speaking of costume.

IX.
Costume

As I have already mentioned, I think that so far much less has been done in this area than in the solution of scenic atmosphere. In spite of the fact that over the past twenty years theatrical costume at first glance seems to have made great advances; in spite of the eye-caressing costume sketches of Bakst, Sideikin, Sapunov, Anisfeld, and others, beautiful in themselves, I contend that the problem of theatrical costume is still infinitely far away from a genuine solution.[1]

Genuine theatrical costume is not finery for the purpose of adorning the actor, it is not a model of the stylish costume of this or that period, it is not a fashion picture from an old journal, and the actor is not a doll or a mannequin, whose chief goal is to show the costume off to advantage. No, the costume is the actor's second skin, it is something inseparable from his essence, it is the visible mask of his scenic figure. It must become so integral a part of him that, just as with the words of a song, not one line may be discarded or changed without at the same time distorting the whole image.

Costume is a new means for enriching the expressiveness of the actor's gesture, for with the help of a genuine costume every acting gesture should acquire special clarity and sharpness or softness and smoothness, depending on its artistic intent. Costume is a means of making the whole body, the whole figure of the actor, more expressive and vibrant, to give it shapeliness and lightness or clumsiness and heaviness in keeping with the scenic figure being created.

Where are these costumes right now?

True, in recent years a series of brilliant sketches has passed before us, from which one can learn the dress of all times and nations (refracted, of course, through the fantasy of the artist), a series of beautiful, colorful compositions, from which one can learn contemporary technique and trends in painting; but there have been practically no genuine theatrical costumes among them. And if you ask the actors—not those to whom smart clothes are more dear than their art, but the few genuine artists—how they feel in the pompous and in themselves very beautiful costumes of the contemporary designers, in the great majority of cases you will hear that the costume does not help but hinders them.

It is for this reason I said that I consider the costumes of *Shakuntala* and *Famira* to be among the most successful solutions of costumes in recent times, because in them the chief role was assigned to the body of the actor, and there was practically no costume at all. But of course this approach has not been sufficiently exploited.

The contemporary artist must find a costume for the actor, one such as those immortal costumes which were found for Harlequin and Pierrot.

Why immortal?

Are they really so beautiful?

No, in this respect they are inferior to many costumes of our artists. Their immortality lies in the fact that they are organically fused with their stage figures; it is as impossible to steal from Harlequin his costume as it is to strip him of his skin. Indeed, if you call to mind the figure of Harlequin, you will see that that indefatigable squabbler, that pugnacious adventurer must by his very nature have such a costume as would cover his whole body like a glove, making it possible for the brilliant fireworks of his rapid, sharp, kaleidoscopic movements to display themselves with ease.

On the other hand, the costume of Pierrot, that handsome white costume with the long sleeves which make Pierrot's arms look like the limbs of a weeping willow—is it not bound up organically with the very core of the character of Pierrot, that sad lover and poet with his soft, flowing movements, now creeping indolently about the earth, now rising weakly toward the sky?

These are the costumes from which one must take inspiration in constructing scenic costume.

I am not at all suggesting that we restore them. The characters of the contemporary theatre and the theatre of the future are much more complicated than Pierrot and Harlequin, and the costumes for them must of course be different, but they must be constructed according to the same sure principle—the principle of harmony with the dynamic essence of the scenic figure being created by the actor.

This principle must be primary. All the other elements—style, period, way of life, etc.—must give way to it, entering into the basic motif only as an accompaniment.

Strange as it may seem, even in the formlessness of contemporary life there is one costume which is organically fused with its character. I refer to the costume of the pilot or the racing driver. Indeed, is not this costume, with gaiters on the legs, with leather jacket and riding breeches, with its billed cap to protect from sun and wind, and with its half-mask of goggles, allowing one to see far ahead at extremely high speeds—is it not intrinsically fused with the man of our electro-machine age?

In order to create a genuine theatrical costume, the artist must here also relinquish the sketch. Here, when one has the skill, it is so simple to draw an interminable cloak that floats beautifully on the breeze, but which, alas, hangs pitifully on the figure of the actor, because he cannot execute over and over again for a period of several hours that one movement which causes the cloak to float with the beautiful lines depicted in the sketch.

Here, too, we must turn to the model. Only a miniature figure of the actor (and the specific actor at that) is sufficient to help the artist work out a theatri-

"Phaedra": the costume itself

Vesnin: costume sketch for "Phaedra"

cal costume in true fashion. Experiments along this line recently carried out in the work of the Kamerny Theatre (costume models by B. Ferdinandov for *Adrienne Lecouvreur*—especially the costumes of Adrienne and Michonet) corroborate this idea completely.* And besides, it is necessary for the artist to know something, however little, of body structure, otherwise he will surely fail to take anatomy into account.

One must never forget, you see, that the costume must fit the actor and not vice versa.

It is time at last to retrieve this simple truth from the dust of oblivion and take it into account, if only a little bit, in creating costumes for the stage. Of course, this does not mean that scenic costume must fit the figure of the actor like his morning coat. It means only that one must count on his figure assuming the freest, most peculiar and fantastic positions, because it—as you of course know, if you are an artist—is the chief material of his art.

Presenting the artist with such important tasks, I am confirming at the same time, I hope, my assertion that I consider his creative participation in the theatre indispensable. And of course Gordon Craig was again wrong in suggesting that the director should also do the work of the artist. Each has more than enough work of his own, and in order not to do it in dilettante fashion, in order to be genuine masters each in his own art, a lifetime is barely sufficient.

Attempts to unite artist and director in one person have invariably come to a sad end. I shall cite two examples.

In the first one, the director wanted to be artist. I refer to Komissarzhevsky's production of *The Tempest*. The result was the complete absence of a unified artistic composition, an amateurishly worked-out scenic platform, Caliban's costume taken from Craig, and other costumes which were in keeping neither with him nor with their respective characters.

In the second, the artist wished to become director. I refer to Benoit's Pushkin production.[2] One need recall this production only dimly to be convinced that if one may debate whether or not Benoit the artist had done a good job, the fact that Benoit the director was absolutely helpless, destroying even the good things Benoit the artist had contributed, is beyond argument.

So it has been, and so it will be, for art does not tolerate dilettantism, and dilettantism is inevitable when one strives to overextend one's capacity.

Kozma Prutkov knew this long ago.[3]

*I must also cite several costumes, exceptionally successful in their conformity to character, by G. Yakulov in *Princess Brambilla* (for instance, Celionati, Bescani, Giglio, the Negroes, etc.).

"Adrienne Lecouvreur"

Costume models for "Giroflé-Girofla"

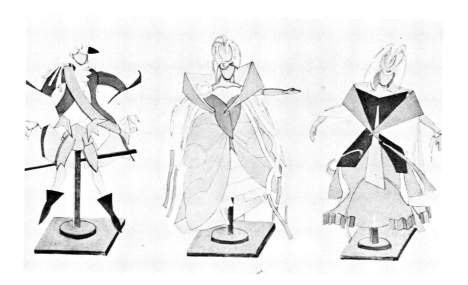

Ferdinandov: costume models for "Adrienne Lecouvreur"

With the solution of the scenic atmosphere for a given production the preparatory process of the director's art ends, and he passes on to the most important, joyful, and exciting portion of his art—the work with his actors.

I already said a good deal about what this work consists of when I spoke about the art of the actor, because in every stage of the actor's work the director invariably acts as his companion and helpmate. The work of the director and actor can produce genuine theatrical art only if they are creatively inseparable—only if from the very first steps of his "scholastic life" as a student of acting the actor has learned to empathize with the director and the director with the actor. Otherwise they have no business on the same stage together; otherwise there is no esprit de corps, and that means no theatre.

Everything I have discussed so far represents all in all a great and complicated artistic process, which precedes the creation of every production. The result is that complete, monolithic work of theatrical art which the spectator perceives during the performance.

X.

The Spectator

The spectator! Without a doubt, no art devotes so much attention to him as does the art of the theatre. And even in our art, never have so many impassioned debates, speeches, and articles been dedicated to him as recently.

Such exceptional concern for the spectator in the theatre unquestionably has great intrinsic significance, since to determine the kind of role the spectator must in essence play in the theatre—either the role of *one who observes* or that of *one who creates*—means to answer to a large degree the question of the whole structure of the contemporary theatre and the theatre of the future. If you conclude that the spectator must play an actively creative role in the theatre, that he be an actual participant in the theatrical action, then you must break the proscenium, carry the action into the auditorium, bring the spectator onto the stage, etc., etc. If you are convinced that the spectator must not be an actively creative element but only an observer, however creative he may be, then the whole structure of the theatre will undoubtedly be completely different. Therefore, moving toward that new theatre for the realization of which we are all working, we must certainly know the kind of role which will be assigned to the spectator in it.

Among ideologists and theoreticians of the theatre, Vyacheslav Ivanov attaches the greatest significance to the participation of the spectator. He considers that the essential element of the theatre is its *communal nature,* that theatrical activity is essentially communal action, and that the decline of the contemporary theatre is to be explained chiefly by the absence of communion —that the spectator, separated from the stage by the footlights, has become anemic, acting only as a witness to the action being carried out, "and there are no veins which might unite these two separate bodies (actor and spectator) by means of a general circulation of creative energy."*

He suggests that herein lies the chief defect of the contemporary theatre, and until that active role which was once his is returned to the spectator, until the vitalizing pulse of communion beats once more in the theatre, it will be only an "iconostasis, remote and austere, rather than calling everyone together in general festive assembly," and so long as such a condition prevails, the renaissance of the theatre is impossible.

Is this really true?

Is it true that its communal nature is such a distinctive feature of the theatre that with its disappearance the theatre is doomed to inevitable degeneration?

I say no. I suggest that the communal aspect of theatre has never been the distinguishing feature of its being to such an extent. It characterizes a whole raft of other phenomena to an immeasurably greater degree. It appears with greatest strength in religion. In every religious cult, in all kinds of religious rites and processions, communal action plays a dominant role. If you trace religious festivals and processions from deepest antiquity to the present, from popular pagan rites to exclusive Christian cults of various sects, from uninhibited orgiastic services in honor of favorite gods to the official public worship of the ruling churches—you see that all of them in greater or lesser degree are based on communal action.

Then if you turn to the important moments of secular life, to moments of great political or social change, you see that here, too, the power or intensity of this or that revolution has depended to a significant degree on the strength of the communal element in it.

*Vyacheslav Ivanov, "To the Stars." [Vyacheslav Ivanovich Ivanov (1866-1949), symbolist poet, playwright, and aesthetician. His theory of art takes its source in Nietzsche's dichotomy of Apollonian and Dionysian temperaments. Ivanov identified Dionysos with Christ. Thus Christian art, for Ivanov, is Dionysian in nature—frenzied, ecstatic, tragic. He was by this route led logically to the conclusion that the theatre was the greatest of the arts, and he agitated for a return of the theatre to such forms as the medieval mysteries, where, he asserted, there was no separation between actors and audienc , but the whole community was fused into a chorus of devotees engaged in an ecstatic religious experience, using the great myths of Christian culture as material for the rites. After the revolution Ivanov worked in the theatre section of Narkompros (People's Commissariat of Enlightenment), and his theories had some influence on the theoreticians of the Proletkult (Proletarian Culture Movement). He soon became disenchanted with the new regime, however, went to Italy, and was converted to Catholicism.—Translator.]

The pulse of communal action invariably beats also in authentic folk festivals, in the marvelous Italian carnivals, and in thousands of amphitheatres
during bullfights.

Thus, while being unquestionably characteristic of a whole line of phenomena of the human spirit, communal action is at the same time least of all characteristic of the theatre. On the contrary, when it does appear, it is a destructive rather than constructive element.

In 1830, at the Theatre Monnaie in Brussels, the play *La Muette* was being
performed. In the middle of the performance, when the words "Love for the
Fatherland is holy" rang out on the stage, the revolutionary enthusiasm which
they evoked on the stage was communicated to the auditorium. The whole
theatre was united in such powerful transport that all the spectators and actors
left their places, grabbing chairs, benches—everything which came to hand—
and, bursting from the theatre, rushed into the streets of Brussels. Thus began
the Belgian revolution.

There is no doubt that here the spirit of communal action blazed up in
striking fashion in the theatre; here at last "two different bodies [were united]
by a common circulation of creative energy"; here the theatre played the fine
and noble role of torch, kindling the immanent revolutionary flame—but the
performance ceased. The pulse of communal action, having begun to beat in the
theatre, fired the revolution but extinguished theatrical action. And if the sacrificial role played by the Theatre Monnaie during those memorable days is
thrice blessed among the great moments in the development of humanity; in
the creative evolution of theatre art it demonstrated once more that the element of communal action is far from being a vitalizing ferment for the theatre, and the active participation of the spectator will not at all lead to the theatre's renascence.

The yearning for communal action in the theatre is undoubtedly connected
with the appearance at the beginning of the twentieth century of an effort to
resurrect the theatre of antiquity. Concluding his article "Theatre," Vsevelod
Meyerhold writes:

> If the stylized theatre seeks the abolition of scenery placed in the same plane with
> actors and set props [?], if it does not want footlights, subordinates the playing of
> the actor to the demands of rhythmic diction and rhythmic, plastic movement [?],
> if it awaits the revival of dance, *and draws the spectator into active participation
> in the action*—is not such a stylized theatre leading toward a revival of the theatre
> of antiquity? ... Yes.*
>
> *Italics mine.

Here is that idea of reconstruction, that antiquarian urge which has undoubtedly brought a great many theoreticians and practitioners of theatre to that hypertrophy of audience participation in the creative aspect of the theatre, the ideological basis of which is the idea of communal action.

But if we turn even to that classic theatre to which Meyerhold alludes, we realize that it is doubtful whether even it drew the spectator "into active participation in the action," for actually the spectator took an active part only while the classic theatre was still unformed, still not crystallized as a self-contained art.

The spectator did indeed play an active role in the ritual of religious festivals when the theatre was just beginning, but at that time he was not yet in essence a spectator. He was the folk, that chorus of the faithful which in conjunction with the coryphaeus expressed in common religious activity its will toward union with the diety.

The actor as priest and the audience as a chorus of believers—such was the embryonic form of *pre*-classical theatre. But as soon as the theatre began to be aware of itself, as soon as it began to take shape, to form itself into an independent art, it gradually reduced the spectator's participation in its activity, and already in classic tragedy we notice an unquestionable diminishing of the role assigned to the chorus. Already in Aeschylus two actors appear and the chorus' participation in the action is weakened accordingly. Sophocles introduced a third actor, and the chorus changed from an active element into an observing and summarizing one (representing the author more often than the audience), and Euripides, crowning the mighty edifice of classic theatre with his artistry, relegated the chorus to a place of still lesser importance. Indeed, in order to get rid of its gratuitous meddling in the action (to abandon the chorus entirely he would have had to disrupt the established form of ancient tragedy), he often arranged, with the help of this or that character, for the chorus to remain silent.

What does this evolution in the role of the chorus mean? Does it signify a progressive decline in classic tragedy, reaching its low point in the person of Euripides, or, on the contrary, does it represent the flowering of classic tragedy, finding in Euripides its most brilliant practitioner? I suggest the latter.

Every art has experienced a period of incubation, when having not yet found itself, not yet discovered its own independent way, it is dependent on a whole line of essentially extrinsic elements. Just so the art of the theatre had its primordial period of incubation, when it still had not crystallized into a self-contained art but was closely bound up with the religious cults of Dionysos in Hellas and Krishna in India, its roots entangled with those of mythology— when it was still impossible to tell where the orgiastic rites of religion ended and theatrical action began. And then, naturally, the spectator took an active part in the action.

But as the theatre gradually found itself, as it began to find its own directions and laws of development. as the theatre stood more and more apart as an independent artistic phenomenon, active participation of the spectator decreased, for, separated from those elements which were not a part of its essential nature, the theatre began to stand on its own. And that evolution of classic theatre which we see from Aeschylus through Sophocles to Euripides, with its gradual diminishing of the role of the chorus, also shows us that when, with Euripides, the theatre finally found itself and became a self-contained fine art, the active participation of the spectator, which fed on the completely different juices of the religious cult, having nothing to do with theatre as such, had in the end to wither away.

Therefore, I suggest that to demand communal action from the theatre in the twentieth century and to base the whole renascence of the theatre on it means trying to turn back the wheel of theatre art; it means striving to deprive the theatre of independent value, making it an adjunct to some mass ideology or other, religious or social, for without a common ideology there is of course no basis for communal action.

The partisans of communal action in the theatre who have most recently come forth—the rhetoricians of the so-called socialist theatre—know this very well. Presenting communal action anew as the basic element of socialist theatre, they point out that so far the theatre has been unable to develop its communal nature because contemporary society has been split, separated by class warfare and class psychology, and therefore, the audience, consisting of people with different ideologies, have not been susceptible to unification by a "general circulation" and have not been able to manifest themselves in common creative endeavor. Now, as we stand on the road to socialism, as a new nationwide ideology comes into being, grounds for the rebirth of a communal basis in the theatre are emerging once again.

Undoubtedly this argument would be quite conclusive if—if communal action were indeed the distinctive basis of theatre.

But it is not.

The path suggested by the socialist theatre is that same path to restoration of *pre*-classical theatre only with different ideological content.* But the path of restoration is not a creative path. And just as there can be no return to the mask and cothurni once binoculars have been·invented, so there can no longer be a return to the spectator's active participation in scenic action once a self-contained art of the theatre has come into being.

Meanwhile, one of the theorists of the socialist theatre, Kerzhentsev, suggests that the spectator must take an active part not only in the theatrical action of the performance but also in rehearsals and all the work of the theatre.[1]

Of course there is no need to tell people of the theatre that to permit the audience to take part in the rehearsals means to deprive theatrical work of artistic value, for where there is an element of chance, there is no art, and the participation of the audience in rehearsals as well as performance will inevitably introduce a substantial element of chance, intruding into the orderliness of scenic action and often plunging it into a chaos from which there is no escape.

In order to show graphically how destructive is the effect of the spectator's intrusion into the course of scenic action, I shall cite an event which took place in the Moscow Art Theatre. Gorki's *Children of the Sun* was playing there, in the third act of which a pogrom takes place on the stage. During the first performance of the play, the audience, electrified by the lifelikeness of the pogrom being carried out on stage, "took part in the action," jumping from the seats and raising such a racket with shouts, hysterics, and chaos, that they had to lower the curtain and cut the act short.[2]

Another example, still more indicative, ended in tragedy. In America, in Chicago in 1909, the famous American actor William Butts was playing Iago. At that moment when the perfidious Iago is inflaming Othello to wild jealousy with his villainous fabrications and inciting him to the murder of Desdemona, a shot rang out unexpectedly from the parterre and William Butts fell to the stage dying. When the excitement died down, it turned out that an American army officer had fired the shot, having lost his head over the shameless conduct of Iago. Learning that William Butts was dead, the officer shot himself on the spot.

The Americans, knowing how to make a sensation even out of death, buried them with great ceremony in one grave, topped by a monument with the following inscription: *"To the ideal actor and the ideal spectator."*[3] You may think what you like, but if there are many such ideal spectators, instead of theatres there will soon be graveyards everywhere.

*That is, that period when the theatre was as yet unformed as an independent art.

I assume these examples demonstrate eloquently enough what that notorious participation of the spectator in the performance leads to. But apparently tradition possesses such invincible hypnotic power that even the *futurists,* who overturn all the age-old principles with such brio, nevertheless turn out to be duped by the very traditions against which they raise their bloodless barricades. The ideologist and leader of the Italian futurists, Marinetti, extolling the music hall in his manifesto about theatre, writes:

> The music hall is the only theatre which *utilizes the collaboration of the public.* *
> The audience does not attend *passively,* like a bored observer, *but participates boisterously in the action,* singing, accompanying the orchestra, punctuating the actors' performance with impromptu caprices and odd dialogues. The actors themselves argue in comic fashion with the musicians. The music hall utilizes cigar and cigarette smoke *to fuse the atmosphere of house and stage.* In this way the audience works together with the fantasy of the actors *and the action takes place simultaneously on the stage, in the loges, and in the parterre.* **

And here are the means which Marinetti recommends for achieving such audience participation in the action:

> To catch them by surprise and force the spectators in the parterre, loges and gallery to act, I suggest the following devices: Spread glue on the seats so that the ladies and gentlemen who get stuck evoke general laughter. Naturally they will be paid for their dresses or suits when they leave. Sell the same seat to ten people. Pile-ups, arguments and abusive language will follow. Offer free seats to men or women who are clearly insane, short tempered or eccentric, capable of provoking incredible uproar by pinching women or other eccentricities. Dust the seats with itching or sneezing powder.

At first this may appear ultra-futurist, terribly revolutionary. Thus our half-baked revolutionists of the socialist theatre, apparently "seduced" by this line of thinking, suggested—in their amateurish plans for mass participation of the spectators in the scenarios being worked out in honor of May First—that obstacles be thrown up in the paths of the processions so as to incite them to action, just like Marinetti's powder.

---

*I can imagine what it would have been like if the audience had taken part in the chorus scenes of *Princess Brambilla,* where every instant is artistically studied, where those taking part in the rhythmic structure on the stage simultaneously dance, sing, juggle, perform acrobatics, etc.

** Italics mine. [A Russian translation of Marinetti's *Manifestoes of Italian Futurism (Manifesty ital'ianskogo futurizma)* was published in Moscow in 1914.—Translator.]

Alas, one need only scratch this arch-futurism a little to reveal our same old gray-haired acquaintance, communal action.

And so even Marinetti has not been able to free himself from the mesmerism of tradition. He has become the favorite model of the revolutionary steeped in that enthusiasm for restoration which unquestionably lies at the base of all attempts to return to the theatre its communal nature, making the spectator an active participant in the action. And if Vyacheslav Ivanov speaks of communal action which must be evoked as an organic basis, Marinetti recommends its use as a mechanical device; and the current socialist "reformers" of the theatre, depending on their personal taste, elect now one now the other path.

In my view the famous concept of "preparatory action," which the genius Scriabin[4] was working on, is on a completely different plane. He also dreamed of the communal participation of the spectator, but with that insight of the genuine artist which was so intrinsic a part of his nature, he gave to it a precisely ordered character. In order to be admitted to the "action," the spectator had to be a specially prepared "initiate," he had to be robed in special dress, etc., etc.

If you examine Scriabin's artistic goals, refracting them through the prism of pure theatrical art, you will see that in the end there was to have been achieved not an action with the active participation of the *spectator,* but action with the orderly, previously rehearsed participation of the *masses* without any elements of chance whatever—masses which, in fact, had *ceased to be spectators* and had become *participants* in the action, just as they had to a lesser degree in productions with *large mass scenes* (for instance Reinhardt's *Oedipus Rex*).

Every *orderly* attempt to enlist the spectator's participation must inevitably come to this: owing to the strength of the fundamental nature of theatrical art, they turn into participants (bad ones in my view), and those *genuine* spectators, who come to see the performance without previous preparation, remain just that, spectators, i.e., not participants but *observers*. That communal participation of the spectator, about which the ideologists of the socialist theatre dream, is possible not in the theatre but in *folk festivals,* which, of course, are also characterized to a greater or lesser degree by an element of theatricalism.

It is not without reason that N. N. Evreinov has long dreamed of the *theatricalization of life* [5] And if the time has now come for genuine national festivals, for carnivals, for spontaneous and joyful playacting, then of course we, masters of theatre, are the first to welcome them and to help them insofar as they touch upon our many-faceted art. But we must have firm knowledge that the means of the theatre, as a self-contained art, are on a completely different level and in different artistic systems.

These are the means of the *theatricalization of the theatre.*

The ideologists of communal action, erroneously eyeing the theatre, must understand this once and for all. True, the role of the spectator in the theatre differs from that which he plays in observing other arts. Very likely it is this seductive aspect thanks to which the ideologists of communal action are directing their gaze to the theatre. But as we have just seen, this role arises from unique causes, rooted in the unique nature of theatre art as such. Indeed, in every other art, the spectator perceives its product after the entire creative process has been completed, after the work has been separated from its creator and has become an independent artistic phenomenon. Thus in painting the spectator sees a finished picture, and he has, essentially, nothing to do with the artist and his creative process; in sculpture—a completed statue; in architecture—a finished temple or palace, etc. And only in the theatre is the spectator present during the actual creative process of the actor, being as it were an eyewitness to the creative process of the performance.

And it is because of that very uniqueness, already pointed out, that the theatre is placed in a unique situation: it is as if its creations are born with the rising of the curtain and cease to exist when it falls, and therefore by their very nature demand the presence of the spectator as it were during the process of their creation and not just upon their completion. It also presents the possibility of assigning to the spectator in the theatre a role different than in any other art.

But there is an undoubted misunderstanding concealed here, which will become evident as soon as you penetrate beneath the at-first-glance deceptive appearance of the superficial fact. You yourself know very well that by the time the play reaches the spectator, all the creative work of the theatre has been essentially completed. You know also that the creative process of the produced play consists of those preparatory tasks—devising the scenario, the characters, the rhythm of the production, its atmosphere, etc., etc.—and in those multitudinous rehearsals and final run-throughs for make-up, costume, lights, set, which continue until the entire collective creative process of the theatre is completed. Therefore, when a given production is unveiled before the spectator, it is of course an already complete, monolithic, self-contained work of theatrical art.*

The difference here, with respect to other arts, consists only in the fact that theatre art, because of its material and its dynamic nature, is perceived not in a static but a dynamic condition. In the theatre every form, fired in the efficacious flame of performance, invariably gives birth to another form, in its turn doomed to death beforehand for the conception of still another—and therefore, in order to display itself, the theatre art *demands that the spectator be right there, at the moment of its dynamic exposure, and not after it.* Consequently, here, too, as in the other arts, the spectator *observes* an already *completed work of art,* but an art *which reveals itself in a different* form than the others—dynamic and not static.

It is also mistaken to think that theatre art is lost without an audience, that the audience is an indispensable impulse to the actor. We all know that sometimes in the working process there occur rehearsals so inspired that no subsequent performance can compare with them. And the performance itself does not at all cease to exist as a work of art if there is no audience in attendance, just as the beautiful statue of the sculptor would not cease to be an art work if he should keep it locked up. It is only that the peculiar characteristics of the *material* of theatre art, the perishability and transitory nature of the human body, set special time limits, due to which the completed scenic work, if it does not wish to remain unknown, must display itself to the spectator at once and not after several years. But the spectator is necessary to it not at all as an actively creative element but only as an observer.

Since this is so, the spectator must be assigned the same role in the theatre as in other self-respecting arts. He must remain a spectator, not a participant.

Therefore, we must repudiate once and for all the attempts at restoration which have been carried out in recent years by the "innovators" of the contemporary theatre. Bridges over the orchestra, actors in make-up running through the parterre, leaving the stage and going into the audience, create not communal action but nonsense and chaos. Fortunately, the spectator tactfully remains a spectator, but extras, in theatrical make-up and costume, appearing

*Of course this does not mean that during performances the actor only reproduces mechanically the already created character. No, the damnation and joy of his art is that he creates his ephemeral forms anew with every performance. But this process is a performing, not a creative art.

together with the public, simply insult the theatre, turning it into an anti-artistic muddle.

So, long live the footlights!

Long live the footlights, which separate the stage from the auditorium, for the stage is a complex and difficult keyboard which only a master-actor can command, but the auditorium is an amphitheatre, designated for the *spectator, who is observing the art of the actor*. To assign the spectator another place, to turn the stage into a "low, altar-like scaffold," onto which, as Meyerhold writes, "it is so easy to run in ecstasy to join in the service," means to pull the theatre back, to try to drag it down from the level of a self-contained art which it took so long to achieve.

But in saying "long live the footlights" I do not, of course, mean to say that I accept the *actual* contemporary footlights with their flat illumination, that I am satisfied with a stage house in which, thanks to the traditional architecture of theatre buildings, beautiful and daring ideas often perish.

Along with the new construction of the scenic platform, there must be a reconstruction of the entire theatre building as well. We have already begun the appropriate experimental work. But however the theatre building may be reconstructed, that invisible barrier about which I am speaking must without fail remain, for we did not promulgate the theatricalization of the theatre, we did not proclaim an acting mastery answerable to its own set of values, we did not throw off the yoke of literature and painting only to fall under the yoke of the auditorium.

In that case, what kind of role do I assign to the spectator in the theatre?

Certainly I do not want him to take the theatre as though it were life. That goes without saying. Nor do I wish the spectator, as Meyerhold writes, contradicting himself, "never for a moment to forget that before him is an actor who is performing,"* No, I have no wish to be like the Hoffmann machinist who steadfastly beats the spectator on the head as soon as he forgets that he is in the theatre.

True, the spectator need not actively participate in the performance, but he must view it *creatively,* and if, on the wings of a fantasy awakened in him by the art of the theatre, he is carried beyond its walls into the wondrous land of Urdar, then I wish him a delighted *bon voyage.*

I desire only that the *fine art of the actor* serve as his magic carpet on that enchanted trip and not the illusory deception of some fairy or magic lantern,

*How then can he "run onto the stage in ecstasy in order to join in the service"?

which are in essence just as alien to the genuine art of the theatre as the fraud of verisimilitude.

It is customary at the end of a book to add a conclusion. I would rather not resort to this custom, since my notes are of course not concluded with the publication of this book. These are only the first pages of those notes which I shall continue to make as long as I work, as long as I am able to test all my ideas and discoveries in the active construction of a theatre; and in this way, the dynamic way of the theatre, I shall derive those experience-tempered principles, laws, and formulas which, perhaps, will make it possible for me or for others more capable to lay if only the first stones of that beautiful and to us indispensable edifice whose name is—*The Science of Theatre Art.*

I believe deeply that such a science must emerge and place our art at last on that firm foundation, from which it may make its flights into creative work confidently, without risk of being dashed to pieces or being absorbed into the territory of contiguous, maybe closely allied, but nevertheless different arts.

A whole series of arts already have their own science, or at least some firm beginnings of it.

Now it is the theatre's turn.

But in order that this science have a suitable base for its construction and development, it is necessary that theatre art at last get an accurate picture of itself and dissociate itself from all attendant elements, it is necessary to carry out resolutely and completely the *theatricalization of the theatre.*

Theatre is theatre.

It is high time we learned this simple truth once and for all.

Its strength is in the dynamism of scenic action.

The One who acts is the Actor.

His strength is in the mastery of his craft.

The Mastery of the Actor is the highest, the true *substance* of the theatre.

The emotional saturation of that mastery is the key to its dynamism.

The Scenic Figure is the Form and essence of its expression.

The rhythm of action is its organizational basis.

And so, the Theatre is Theatre.

And there is only one way to make this seeming truism become a joy-giving fact.

That way is through the *Theatricalization of the Theatre.*

1915-1920

Notes

For Translator's Introduction

1 Lucie R. Sayler, "Stanislavsky to His Players," *Theatre Arts Monthly* (January, 1923), 37. This is a transcript of Stanislavsky's lecture to the Moscow Art Theatre company at the beginning of its work on *The Bluebird*.

2 Constantin Stanislavsky, *My Life in Art* (Boston, 1924), 568.

3 *Ibid.*, 383-84.

4 It is important to remember here that this discussion concerns Stanislavsky and the Moscow Art Theatre at the time Tairov was writing his notes—long before Stanislavsky published *An Actor Prepares* and *Building a Character*. It is in no way meant to describe the Stanislavsky theory of theatre as it can now be studied from his complete works written during a lifetime of unceasing experiment which did not end until 1938.

5 Vladimir Nemirovich-Danchenko, *My Life in the Russian Theatre* (Boston, 1936), 187.

6 These excerpts were reprinted in Oliver Sayler, *The Russian Theatre Under the Revolution* (Boston, 1920), 215-16.

7 John Martin, "How Meyerhold Trains His Actors," *Hound and Horn* (Fall, 1930), 16.

8 Andre Van Gyseghen, *Theatre in Soviet Russia* (London, 1943), 87.

9 It is interesting to note that in spite of reservations about his style, the government was at this time pouring 200,000 rubles a year into Tairov's acting school alone, and each year there was a list of over eight hundred applicants averaging eighteen years of age, from which only a score were taken.

Chapter I

1 Vera Fyodorovna Komissarzhevskaya (1864-1910), Russian actress and producer. In 1904 she founded the Drama Theatre, which soon gained a reputation as the most progressive theatre in Leningrad. In 1906, after Meyerhold broke with Stanislavsky, she invited the former to continue his experiments in stylized production at her theatre. In 1907 she, too, broke with Meyerhold and resolved to give up the theatre and become a teacher. She died while on tour trying to settle her debts before retiring.

2 Julius Eichenwald (1872-1928), Russian writer and critic of the impressionist school. Eichenwald was a proponent of "art for art's sake," and his article "Otritsanie teatra" (A Denial of Theatre), published in 1912, in which he rejected the theatre as a genuine art form, affirming that it was only a counterfeit of life, stirred up a heated controversy.

3 Fyodor Sologub (Fyodor Kuzmich Teternikov, 1863-1927), a leading symbolist poet, novelist, and playwright. In his article on the theatre, he advocated production techniques which would, as Tairov points out, turn actors virtually into marionettes.

Mikhail Petrovich Artsybashev (1878-1927), a "decadent" writer of the period. His plays and novels were dominated by themes of death and sex, which he considered the only realities.

Ilya Dmitrievich Surguchyov (1881-1956), writer and playwright. His play *Torgovi dom (The Firm)* was produced at the Alexandrinsky in 1913 and the Maly in 1914. *Osennie skripky (Autumn Violins)* was produced by the Moscow Art Theatre in 1915.

4 The Free Theatre was founded by K. A. Mardzhanov in 1913 as a "synthetic" theatre, presenting a wide range of theatrical productions, from tragedy to ballet to light opera. Poor business management and a break between Mardzhanov and his backer, V. V. Sukhodolsky, forced it to close after only one season.

5 Nikolai Fyodorovich Monakhov (1875-1936), an extremely gifted and many faceted actor, equally adept at pantomime, comedy, tragedy, and light opera.

Fyodor Ivanovich Chaliapin (1873-1938), the famous Russian basso.

Davydov: Either the famous Russian tenor Alexander Michailovich Davydov (1872-1944) or Vladimir Nikolaevich Davydov (1849-1925), a well-known actor.

Alice Georgievna Koonen (1889-   ), a young actress from the Moscow Art Theatre. She later married Tairov and, under his direction, became one of the great Russian actresses of the twentieth century.

Maria Fyodorovna Andreeva (1869-1953), former member of the Moscow Art Theatre. She had recently returned to Moscow after six years abroad with Gorky as his secretary and companion.

Baltrushaitis: Possibly Jurgis Baltrushaitis (1873-1945), a symbolist poet of Lithuanian origin. He had translated Ibsen, Hauptmann, and d'Annunzio into Russian.

6 *The Beautiful Elena,* music by Offenbach, libretto by Munstein; *The Yellow Jacket,* by G. C. Hazelton and J. H. Benrimo; *The Sorochintsy Fair,* a comic opera by Musorgsky, based on the short story by Gogol.

All three works were produced during the first and only season of the Free Theatre.

7 *The Veil of Pierrette,* by Arthur Schnitzler with music by P. Donani, was also produced that first season. It was later revived by Tairov in his Kamerny Theatre (October 6, 1916).

8 Georg Fuchs' *Die Revolution des Theaters* had been published in 1909. Meyerhold's *O teatra* was published in 1913.

9 In spite of the feminine ending, perhaps Tairov refers here to Yuri Iosifovich Slonimski (1902-   ), critic, ballet historian, and librettist, who began publishing critical articles in 1919.

10 "Perezhivanie" was a key term in Stanislavsky's teaching and writing. It refers to that "living through" or "emotionally experiencing" the role which was such a vital feature in his system of working up a part.

11   The Russian term used to describe this kind of theatre is "uslovny" (conventional), referring to the use of "conventional" rather than realistic gesture and movement as well as to symbolic use of color and line in costume and scene design. Tairov has particular reference here to the work of Meyerhold.

12 Nikolai Nikolaevich Sapunov (1880-1912), artist and scene designer. He began working with Meyerhold in 1905 at the theatre-studio on Povarskaya Street. He went with Meyerhold to Vera Komissarzhevskaya's theatre in St. Petersburg, designing *The Death of Tintagiles* (Maeterlinck), *Hedda Gabler, Balaganchik* (Blok), and others.

Ivan Ivanovich Sudeikin (1882-1946), artist and scene designer. He first began working as scene designer with Meyerhold at the Komissarzhevskaya theatre in 1906. He later worked for nearly all of the "theatricalist-symbolist" directors: Evreinov, F. F. Komissarzhevsky, Ozarovsky, Diaghilev in Paris, and Tairov himself. (He designed *The Marriage of Figaro* and *Carnival of Life* at the Kamerny.) Sudeikin emigrated to America in 1923, where he designed ballet sets.

13 In *Boris Godunov.*

14 Seeking to create a "synthetic theatre," peopled by "universal actors," F. F. Komissarzhevsky—Vera's brother—started a studio called the New Theatre in 1918. It lasted only one year. He staged there *The Abduction from the Harem*, by Mozart, and *The Tempest*. Komissarzhevsky left the Soviet Union in 1919, writing and working in theatres and theatre schools in Paris, New York, Vienna, and London until his death in 1954.

15 A lake of milk or sometimes a spring which, according to Yakut (Siberian) mythology, flows from beneath the roots of the Tree of Life, which stands at the center of the earth disk. The lake figures as a symbol in Hoffmann's *Princess Brambilla*, which Tairov staged at the Kamerny in 1920. In the present work he makes frequent allusion to characters and events in the Hoffmann tale.

16 Konstantine Dmitrievich Balmont (1867-1943), one of the first Russian symbolist poets and the most popular one of the day.

17 Pavel Varfolomeevich Kuznetsov (1878-   ), painter and scene designer. Kuznetsov later took up directing, staging *Stenka Razin* (1918) and a series of productions at the Moscow State Circus, including *Revolutionary Carrousel* (1920).

18 Sylvain Levi, *Le théâtre indien* (Paris, 1890).

19 *Thamira of the Cither,* a "bacchic tragedy" by Innokenty Annensky, one of the leaders of the Russian symbolist movement. Opened November 2, 1916.

20 Goldoni's *The Fan* was the opening production of the 1915-1916 season. *Princess Brambilla*, a "capriccio" for the theatre, opened May 4, 1920.

21 By Rimski-Korsakov, produced by Diaghilev in Paris, 1914.

22 Opened October 10, 1915.

23 Petipa (1850-1919) was noted as one of the most accomplished technicians of his time. He was a master of physical and vocal expression, could wear a costume from any period with the finesse characteristic of the period; his characterizations were, by report, a veritable filigree of individualizing physical detail. His abilities were a prime example of the technical perfection Tairov demanded of his actors. He left the Kamerny in 1917.

Chapter II

1 Alexander Raphaelovich Kugel (1864-1928), well-known Russian theatre critic. Editor of *Teatr i iskusstvo (Theatre and Art),* 1897-1918.

V. G. Belinsky (1811-1848), leading Russian literary critic and thinker of the 1830's and 1840's. An advocate of "critical realism," he demanded an inner fidelity or truth to life in a work of art.

Chapter III

1 See Chapter I, note 10.

2 The Second Studio was formed in November, 1916, by Stanislavsky and V. L. Mchedelov from former students of an acting school run by N. G. Alexandrov, N. C. Massalitinov, and N. A. Podgorny. *The Green Ring*, by Zinaida Hippius, was selected as its first production because of its suitability to young performers (most of the Second-Studio students were still in their teens). In 1924 the studio was incorporated into the Art Theatre company proper, its young actors becoming, as it were, the second generation of the Moscow Art Theatre.

3 Realism and stylization figured as a theme in much of Briusov's writing on the theatre. In 1907 he gave a lecture, "Theatre of the Future," in various Moscow theatres and halls. The article here cited was published in *Kniga o novom teatre (Book About the New Theatre)*, St. Petersburg, 1908.

Chapter IV

1 Pushkin's *Feast During the Plague, Mozart and Salieri,* and *The Stone Guest* were produced in 1915. Byron's *Cain* was produced in 1920, being the first new production by the Art Theatre after the revolution.

2 By L. Stalitsa. Opened January 23, 1917.

3 *L'art du comédien* (Paris, 1886),2nd ed., Paris, 1894.

4 One of the earliest of the artificially constructed international auxiliary languages, invented about 1879.

5 Vasily Vasilevich Kamensky (1884-1961), a poet and dramatist. He was one of the founding members of the cubo-futurist school in St. Petersburg, and in 1913-1914 traveled around Russia with Mayakovsky and Burlyuk, presenting revolutionary poetry readings. lectures, and speeches. He was much interested in folk lore and folk heroes, and his play, *Stenka Razin,* was one of the fruits of that interest. It was given a highly stylized production in Moscow in 1918, and it is this production to which Tairov refers.

Chapter VII

1 Oscar Wilde's *Salome,* in a translation by Balmont, opened at the Kamerny October 9, 1917. Alexandra Ekster was the designer.

2 Probably the opera by A. Rubinstein, based on the story by Lermontov.

Chapter VIII

1 *La Bayadère,* libretto by Petipa and Khoudekov, music by L. F. Minkus.

2 Alexandra Exter (1884-1949). Though Madame Exter was considered a cubist, she was distinguished by her feeling for the third dimension, her efforts to achieve sculpturesque effects in her painting. She had also been experimenting in the dynamic use of color—color which, applied in rhythmic patterns, might evoke a feeling of movement and action in the viewer. She was, therefore, ideally suited to carry out Tairov's theories of stage design. Her greatest fame as a scenic artist and her major influence on succeeding artists come from her costume designs. She created "dynamic costumes," using variation in material as well as color to create costumes which expressed the distinctive rhythm of each character.

3 Rayonism was a Russian derivative of futurism. It sought to add a fourth dimension to painting by utilizing parallel and crossed beams of light to evoke in the viewer the sensation of breaking through space into time. Its leading proponent was Michael Larrionov, artist and scene designer, and husband of Natalia Goncharova.

4 *Salome* opened October 9, 1917. The incongruity of this production and the revolution which was taking place in the streets outside the theatre was almost prophetic. It was apolitical, highly refined, sensuous—the very antithesis of official Soviet theatre aesthetics as they came to be defined by the end of the first decade of the new regime. From this production until his death in 1950, Tairov was to carry on a running battle with a government which had declared war on "formalism" in the arts.

5 In spite of Tairov's criticism, Komissarzhevsky's staging of the Offenbach opera

became a classic imitated by motion pictures as well as other stage producers. It was first produced at the New Theatre in 1918-1919.

6 *Sleeping Beauty,* music by Tchaikovsky, choreography by Marius Petipa, was first produced in 1890 at the Marinsky Theatre in St. Petersburg. In 1899 the Bolshoi Theatre in Moscow mounted a production. Presumably it is this latter to which Tairov refers.

7 Karl Fyodorovich Valtz (1816-1929), one of the foremost scenic technicians of his time. He worked at the Bolshoi Theatre for sixty-five years (1861-1926) and became famous for his special effects.

8 Alexander von Salzmann, described by Macgowan as one of the greatest authorities on lighting in the European theatre. He worked with Appia and Jaques-Dalcroze at Hellerau before the war. See Kenneth Macgowan, *The Theatre of Tomorrow* (New York, 1921), 190.

9 Aristarkh Vasilievich Lentulov (1882-1943), artist and scene designer. At this time he was associated with the cubist school. He designed *The Merry Wives of Windsor* for Tairov in 1916. In 1918-1919 he designed *Tales of Hoffmann* at Komissarzhevsky's New Theatre.

10 *King Harlequin,* by P. Lotara, opened November 29, 1917, directed by Tairov, designed by B. Ferdinandov.

Chapter IX

1 Lev Samoilovich Bakst (1866-1924), perhaps the most famous of the Russian designers outside Russia. He was a member of the *World of Art* group and gained his great fame as designer for the Russian Ballet in Paris under Diaghilev.

Sudeikin, Sapunov, see Chapter I, note 12.

Boris Izrailevich Anisfeld (1879-   ), another member of the *World of Art* group; he also designed for Diaghilev. He later emigrated to the United States and designed at the Metropolitan and Chicago operas.

2 *Feast During the Plague, The Stone Guest, Mozart and Salieri,* produced at the Moscow Art Theatre in 1915.

3 "Kozma Prutkov" is the pen name under which A. K. Tolstoy and the brothers Zhemchuznikov published a series of humorous articles and nonsense verse in the mid-nineteenth century. The "collected works" appeared in 1884 and still rank among the classics of Russian humor. Prutkov's proverbs and epigrams were particularly popular.

Chapter X

1 Platon Mikhailovich Kerzhentsev (1881-1940), Soviet historian and statesman (Soviet plenipoteniary in Switzerland 1921-1923). He was president of the Committee for Culture of the Soviet of People's Commissars, USSR, 1936-1938.

2 Stanislavsky describes this incident in some detail in *My Life in Art* (New York, 1959), 439-40.

3 I can find no confirmation of this incident.

4 Alexander Nikolaevich Scriabin (1871-1915). A somewhat ecstatic theorizer, Scriabin saw as the spiritual goal of his art the emancipation of the human soul and the achievement of self-expression. In his unfinished work "Mystery," dance, speech, perfume, and color were to be combined in a kind of total theatre ritual using two thousand participants.

5 See N. N. Evreinov, *The Theatre in Life,* trans. Alexander I. Nazaroff (New York, 1927).

Index

acrobatics, 83, 85
actors and acting
    actor's art, 41-42, 45 ff., 50-51, 53, 66 ff.
    actor's creative activity, 71-72, 91 ff.
    actor's external technique, 71, 81 ff.
    actor's internal technique, 71, 73 ff.
    actor's material, 69
    actor's scenic figure, 77 ff.
    actor's scenic image, 77, 78
    actor's training, 26 ff., 31, 63 ff., 70 ff., 82 ff.
Adrienne Lecouvreur, 37, 79, 89, 129
All God's Chillun Got Wings, 37
Andreeva, Maria Fyodorovna, 42
Anisfeld, Boris I., 125
Antigone (Hasenclever), 37
Aristotle, 41
Artsybashev, Mikhail Petrovich, 41
l'Arlesienne, 54
Azure Carpet, The, 83, 88
Bakst, Lev S., 125
ballet, 93-94
Balmont, Konstantin, 57
Baltrushaytis, Jurgis, 42
Beautiful Elena, The, 43, 54
Benoit, A. N., 129
Bernhardt, Sara, 42
Belinsky, V. G., 68
bio-mechanics, 27
Blessed Are Those Who Hunger, 45
Briusov, Valeri, 50, 59, 77
Cain, 82
Carter, Huntly, 17
Chaliapin, Fyodor I., 42

Chekhov, Anton, 99
classic theatre, 135-136
color (on the stage), 123
composer, the, 104 ff.
Copeau, Jacques, 31-32
Coquelin, Constant, 44, 74, 86, 87, 89
costume (for the stage), 58 ff., 125 ff.
Craig, Gordon, 40, 42, 66 ff., 76, 79, 85, 89, 97, 100, 129
communal action, 132 ff.
Dana, H. W. L., 17
Davidov, A. M. [or V. N.], 42
Delsarte, François, 81
Desire Under The Elms, 37
Diaghilev, Serghey, 19
diction, 85 ff.
dilettantism, 67 ff., 100
directing, 90 ff.
director as master, the, 101
director's role, the, 93-95
Donani, E., 43, 51
Duse, Eleanora, 40, 42
dynamics (of the theatre), 141
Eichenwald, Julius, 40, 41, 89
Ekster, Alexandra, 112
emotional form, 52, 53, 65, 77
emotional gesture, 52, 53
Eros and Psyche, 45
Evreinov, N. N., 17, 18, 28, 139
Exchange, The, 35, 65
Famira Kifared, 32, 37, 62, 88, 89, 103, 104, 112, 117, 122, 124, 126
Ferdinandov, B. A., 129
First Studio, 24
footlights, 142

Forterre, Henri, 104
Free Theatre, 21, 42, 52 ff.
Fuchs, Georg, 42, 45
futurism, 138-139
Giroflé-Girofla, 37
Giselle, 78
Gluck, C. W., 104
Golden Cockerel, The, 63
Goldoni, Carlo, 98
Goncharova, Natalia, 63
Green Ring, The, 75
gymnastics, 83
Hairy Ape, The, 37
Hamlet, 45
Heroes, 37
Hoffmann, T. A., 122
Houghton, Norris, 17-18
improvisation, 79-80
Ivanov, Vyacheslav, 132-133
Jessner, Leopold, 32
Kamensky, Vasili, 88
Kamerny Theatre, 34 ff., 55 ff., 117, 118
King Harlequin, 65, 104, 124
Komissarzhevskaya Theatre, 20-21, 25, 40, 48, 62
Komissarzhevsky, F. F., 17, 18, 28, 54, 117, 129
Koonen, Alice Georgievna, 7, 21, 37, 42, 64, 79, 83, 88
Kronegh, Ludwig, 19
Kugel, Alexander R., 67
Kuznetsov, Pavel, 59
La Muette, 134
Lentulov, A., 123
Levi, Sylvain, 59-60, 69
light (for the stage), 123
literature in the theatre, 96 ff.
Lunacharsky, Anatol, 35
Machinal, 36
Maeterlinck, Maurice, 19
Man Who Was Thursday, The, 36
Mardzhanov, K. A., 21, 43, 51, 53
Marinetti, F. T., 138
Marriage of Figaro, The, 104
master-actor, 91, 99
Meyerhold, V. E., 17, 18, 19, 20, 24 ff., 28, 33-34, 40, 45, 47 ff., 59, 78, 86, 98, 134
Mobile Theatre, 21, 45
model, the, 106-108
Moland, Louis, 98
Molière, 98

Monakhov, Nikolai F., 42
Moscow Art Theatre, 20, 22 ff., 53
music, 103-105
Natalya Tarpova, 36
Nemirovich-Danchenko, V. I., 18, 22 ff.
neo-model, 109 ff., 118 ff.
neo-realism, 65, 115
New Theatre, 54
O'Neill, Eugene, 36
Optimistic Tragedy, The, 37
Order of Lenin, 37
Orpheus, 104
pantomime, 43-44
Pavlova, 78
"perezhivanie," 45 ff., 73 ff.
Petipa, Marius M., 64, 69
Petty Bourgeois, 46
Phaedre, 37
Pichel, Richard, 101
playwright's text, the, 97 ff.
Princess Brambilla, 37, 63, 84, 85, 100, 103, 104, 124, 138
"Proclamations of an Artist," 35
Prutkov, Kozma, 129
Purple Island, The, 36
Pushkin, Alexander S., 52
rayonism, 118
realism, 19, 28 ff., 44 ff., 73 ff., 92
Reinhardt, Max, 42
rhythm, 32-33, 103-105
Romeo and Juliet, 97
Salome, 37, 65, 103, 120
Salvini, Tommaso, 42
Sapunov, Nikolai N., 48, 125
Sarochintsy Fair, The, 43, 54
Saylor, Oliver, 17
scenic atmosphere, 31, 106 ff.
scenic forms, 114 ff.
scenic platform, the, 110 ff.
Scriabin, Alexander N., 139
Second Studio, 75
settings, 59-60, 63
Shakuntala, 37, 56 ff., 126
Shchepkin, Mikhail Semenovich, 19
Sister Beatrice, 49
sketch, the, 108 ff.
Sleeping Beauty, 122
socialist theatre, 136-137
Sologub, F., 41, 100
spectator, the, 132 ff.
speech dynamics, 89
speech rhythm, 87-89

St. Joan, 37
St. Petersburg, 40
Stanislavsky, Konstantin, 17, 18, 19, 20, 22 ff., 28
Stenka Razin, 88
Stroganov Academy, 117-118
stylization, 28 ff., 47 ff., 93
Sudeikin, Ivan Ivanovich, 48, 125
Sulerzhitsky, Leopold Anton, 24
Surguchev, Ivan, 41
symbolism, 19, 24
"synthetic" theatre, 21-22, 28, 34 ff., 54
Tairov, Alexander, 20-22, 28 ff., 33 ff.
Tales of Hoffmann, 122

The Demon, 104
The Fan, 63
Theatres of October, 27
theatre-studio, 19, 48
theatricality, 25-26, 139-140, 143
Tidings Brought to Mary, The, 35
Toy Box, The, 65
d'Udin, Jean, 87, 104
Vakhtangov, Eugene, 17, 18, 28
Van Gyseghen, André, 17, 35
Veil of Pierrette, The, 43, 52, 53, 54
voice, the, 85 ff.
Yakulov, G., 129
Yellow Jacket, The, 43, 53, 54

S10085